AFFIRMATIONS
of the LIGHT
in TIMES *of* DARKNESS

AFFIRMATIONS
of the LIGHT *in*
TIMES *of* DARKNESS

Healing Messages from
a Spiritwalker

A Sacred Planet Book

LAURA AVERSANO

Inner Traditions
Rochester, Vermont

Inner Traditions
One Park Street
Rochester, Vermont 05767
www.InnerTraditions.com

Text stock is SFI certified

Sacred Planet Books are curated by Richard Grossinger, Inner Traditions editorial board member and cofounder and former publisher of North Atlantic Books. The Sacred Planet collection, published under the umbrella of the Inner Traditions family of imprints, is comprised of works on the themes of consciousness, cosmology, alternative medicine, dreams, climate, permaculture, alchemy, shamanic studies, oracles, astrology, crystals, hyperobjects, locutions, and subtle bodies.

Cataloging-in-Publication Data for this title is available from the Library of Congress

ISBN 978-1-64411-271-7 (print)
ISBN 978-1-64411-272-4 (ebook)

Printed and bound in the United States by Lake Book Manufacturing, Inc. The text stock is SFI certified. The Sustainable Forestry Initiative® program promotes sustainable forest management.

10 9 8 7 6 5 4 3 2 1

Text design and layout by Priscilla Baker
This book was typeset in Garamond Premier Pro with Avant Garde, Thirsk, and Hermann used as display typefaces

To send correspondence to the author of this book, mail a first-class letter to the author c/o Inner Traditions • Bear & Company, One Park Street, Rochester, VT 05767, and we will forward the communication, or contact the author directly at **www.LauraSilvanaAversano.com.**

CONTENTS

FOREWORD

Richard Grossinger

Laura arrived in my reality mysteriously a couple of days after Sacred Planet Books, a collection I am curating under the umbrella of Inner Traditions, was christened. I discovered her on Facebook, or thought I did. I qualify that by reminding readers that spirits use all available forms—poltergeists, electrical wires, software, cryptids, tricksters, even imposters—to announce their presence. Whereas Laura does not usually "friend" strangers, I *do* accept most friend requests as a writer and publisher. Yet for me to notice an unknown friend's posts immediately and then take them seriously as authentic real-time transmissions is rare. Laura's statements touched me at a soul level. These weren't mass communications or Facebook idylls; they shot off the screen.

Another point here: Laura's Facebook image is beautiful and soulful, otherworldly or meta-worldly. Her gaze, active in its stillness, crosses domains and spheres of being. She transmits vulnerability and innocence but also a Shiva-like witnessing of what this world has done. That look has experienced betrayal, violence, genocide, evil and darkness, yet is praising the Divine. It is ancient, worn, fierce, not virginal or guileless. It is the female side of Creation, binding its wounds with the freshness of spring. That is not beauty so much as innate, faery-embodied spirit—part plant energy, part hominid.

The night after I read one of Laura's guidings through the abyss, I awoke in terror at an intruding entity or energy—only to see not her image, not to *see* at all, but to feel a protecting energy around me. It was not a coverlet or cocoon. It was moving toward the unknown, impelling my soul with it and giving me a sense of safety and hope. I recognized Laura as anima and guide.

Reaching to the figure beyond its Facebook identity, I asked her for a psychic reading per her vocation—she calls them intuitive sessions. I didn't know then who was behind the profile, if she even was a woman as opposed to the other possibilities. After all, anyone could have written those words and dispatched them behind a stock photo of Tolkien's Arwen.

She said that we would not do a psychic reading—or its equivalent in her system—but that we would work together on other projects and she would transmit the energy I needed in the course of them.

I discovered that she lived in pretty much the last place I expected, not far from where I grew up in New York City.

She was also not a publishing or public neophyte. But none of her prior books had led to a public arc in keeping with her stature, for she is really one of our times' guides and avatars, a different energy from Marianne Williamson or Pema Chödrön but on a par. In any case, my job was to figure out her reentry and second debut.

Eighteen years before I began to work on this book, Laura Aversano was a full-fledged medical intuitive and Christian mystic. She was courted by agents, producers, and publishers, with possibilities of her own television show. None of it panned out, so Laura stuck to her real work: her healing practice. For decades since, she has treated clients at her home and by long distance.

Laura's initial publishing launch was marked by four books, though the first was the same text in two formats. *The Divine Nature of Plants: Wisdom of the Earth Keepers*, a lovely edition with color plates, was published in 2002 by Swan Raven & Co. in North Carolina. Thirty-two years old then, Laura was writing from her direct connections with the spirits of each plant. She was not psychoactive in an entheogenic sense, but she was eliciting healing secrets from plant consciousnesses by calling to their spirits and summoning them out of etheric and astral realms from the energy, signature, and paraphysical matrix of each—angelica and astragalus to wormwood and yarrow. These intuitive diagnoses were later confirmed by traditional herbal pharmacopeia.

The Divine Nature of Plants ended its run with Swan Raven and was later reissued by Llewellyn Publications in Minnesota, where it was edited, retitled, and rereleased in 2009 as *Plant Spirit Journey*. In this version, she added accounts of how she received the various properties from plant spirits—describing a shaman's journey and all that it embraces. A third version of this material will be published within the Sacred Planet Books collection.

I had initially read Laura's posts as New Agey, but I soon realized that they were coming from an older, more archetypal source, more like the Psalms, the Gospel of Luke, Plotinus, or fragments of Heraclitus. Yet her voice transcends genre or affiliation; it is one that has convened and conversed with spirit, that lives between worlds and states of embodiment and so *is* a spirit too. She is not influenced (beyond secondary countercultural context) by channeling, abundance, "create your own reality," Paganism, Gnosticism, Wicca, the Aquarian Age, or entheogens.

Laura's essential training is, astonishingly, in the old Church, *that* one, the one that leads to the Vatican. She brings the skills and frequencies of an exorcist and demonologist as well as of a medicine woman, medium, and bodyworker. That is why she conducts a subtle, dense energy and mature wisdom—that and her natural gifts. She was formally ordained in the other side of the religious spectrum.

Her participation in esoteric Christianity resonates through her Sicilian forebears—she is first-generation New World, and she incarnated at a critical three-century juncture in this lineage, so she carries its ancestral weight.

In 2001, before any of Laura's plant work was published, she began receiving another locution, *The Light of God.* In her own words, "Before the dictation of *The Light of God* actually began, the spiritual process of understanding my own relationship to the light and the darkness had been taking place for a very long time. In my prayers, the spirits that have been guiding me told me of a book that I was going to write, or rather, that they were going to dictate to me. I had no conscious awareness of the content, but I had faith in the importance of the work that was to come.

"The dictation began in the year 2001. . . . It began with light. Then it was followed by darkness. And then the words came. And they came to me and they came through me; in many ways, and on many levels. From the time I listened to the time I wrote them down, the voice of God became a process. This process raised me up to different realms in the world of spirit. It brought with it ecstatic mystical experiences of the Divine as well as challenged me on the earth plane both physically and mentally."

Laura self-published *The Light of God* in 2003, a dense weaving of sacred tongues and metalinguistic vibrations. It is filled with multiple levels of discourse, parallel and overlapping voices, biblical interpretations, and primary ontological issues and polarities within the Christian gnosis. It is no exaggeration to call it a combination of apocrypha and *A Course in Miracles* with chords of The Book of Mormon and *Oahspe*.

The Light of God is the only dictation Laura has published. Another dictation, as yet unpublished and about half its length, came to her as "The Nature of Evil." (I hope to see it on a future Sacred Planet list.) Its vibration radiates through *Affirmations of the Light in Times of Darkness,* the elucidation of darkness as a way of God.

At the beginning of "The Nature of Evil," Laura writes: "With some understanding of human relationship and the potential for it to serve mankind, we strive to understand the nature of evil, the responsibility of each participant, and the responsibility of God. We must first recognize that our search for this understanding is only present because we seek to know God in all His truth. God has always been representative of the light. Evil has always been representative of the darkness. We are as much of the light as we are of the darkness. It is for this simple reason that we desire to know what evil is and why it exists. In looking for these answers, we must reflect deeply on our relationship to the Divine, the relationship we have to others, and primarily, the relationship we have with ourselves. If we are looking to define evil by searching externally, we are missing the opportunity to fully understand and embrace its nature. When we begin to explore these precepts, we will acquire the knowledge necessary to interpret the nature of evil differently from how we have been. We will begin to see how both the light and the darkness of God work co-creatively to support human potential and spiritual growth. . . .

"I am here to guide you into the nature of evil, into the nature of yourself, and into the nature of God."

I hope that you get by now why Laura Aversano's affirmations are not your everyday New Age credos or an Aquarian version of the Andrews Sisters' "Pack up your troubles in your old kit bag / And smile, smile, smile."

She speaks from the heart of Creation, the heart of danger, the depth of the Divine in all of its excruciating, ecstatic contradiction.

This provides Divine solace in the face of darkness, grief, suffering, and separation from God, in the face of COVID and civilizational dissolution. Laura can't do it alone, but with God, she holds space.

Stop and consider how profound that is: *HOLD SPACE*. The space is our own, but she can hold it.

I experienced this once when we were talking on the phone. "Feel that," she suddenly said, "do you feel how it just shifted?" What had changed was the motion of the tree outside, the sunlight, the texture of the air—silence, sound, and the nature of being.

When a friend did a session with Laura at my suggestion, she found her actual words mundane, generic to a woman her age, and was about to blow them off. Within hours, something so extreme it was unimaginable happened. It wasn't just an internal shift; it was an actual thing in her social and professional world.

She was astonished. "How did you do that?!" she called to

the non-present Laura. While Laura had been engaging her attention with meanings, she was holding silent space for her energetically. And then the world changed.

So it will be when you encounter the affirmations, lessons, prayers, mottos, vibrations, and locutions in this book. Do not go at them as honey or candy or radiance; do not take them as *anything*. Let them hold space for you; then claim your space within their vibration.

RICHARD GROSSINGER is the curator of Sacred Planet Books, a member of the Inner Traditions editorial board, the founder and former publisher of North Atlantic Books, and a founding copublisher of *Io,* a seminal interdisciplinary literary journal that ran from 1964 to 1993. He attended Amherst College and completed a Ph.D. in ecological anthropology at the University of Michigan. He has written more than thirty widely acclaimed books on alternative medicine, cosmology, embryology, and consciousness, including *Dark Pool of Light: Reality and Consciousness, The Night Sky: Soul and Cosmos,* and *Bottoming Out the Universe.*

PREFACE

I was born in a lineage of seers and what I call spiritwalkers. Transcending time and space while interacting within the spirit world and unconscious states of humanity seemed like my birthright from the moment I came into this world.

When I was little, I would play in the alcove atop my bedroom closet. I often used to think that I was dreaming while awake, since I would see and speak with people that no one else in the house seemed to notice. Alternate realities, various lifetimes, and prior incarnations became my vocabulary, my blueprint for existing, even as a child so young. I remember telling my mom about my special friends who would visit and play with me. By the time I was six or seven, I had developed a keen interest in the afterlife and in souls who could speak and connect with us from beyond the veil. I remembered lives I'd lived before and told my mom how I'd died in some of them— and how I persevered in others. Names from history would cross my lips when I was still learning how to read. My curiosity about ESP was strong, and I hungered to know more about crossing the veil, time travel, and how to move to and from dimensions. I became fascinated with mysticism even though I didn't refer to it in the appropriate vernacular. I was raised Catholic and was very keen on understanding the healing abilities of Christ and the saints. I thought my interests were the same as my friends, but I realized very quickly in second grade, when I began speaking of such things, that perhaps I should keep quiet.

My mother became my guide in this world. She held space for my growing abilities, sometimes consciously and sometimes not. She later shared stories with me about how she would protect me from spirits that she felt came to bring harm to one so innocently young.

My mother was raised in Sicily. Her maiden name translated from Latin means "one star."

She too was born a vessel for healing through her ability to see beyond the present.

As a young child, she would awaken in the middle of the night to see the Holy Mother standing at the foot of her bed. Most of the time she thought she was dreaming. Her visitations became my visitations.

She remembers traversing the streets of Sicily praying, and sometimes people would follow. There is even a story that my mother appeared to have died. She collapsed with no apparent heartbeat and was prepared in burial clothes and placed in the middle of her childhood home for visitors to come and pay their respects. Some time had passed, and she woke up as people were praying over her body to the shock of onlookers and family. Stories like this run in my family—mysterious illnesses brought on by spiritual manifestations, many of which have impacted my own physicality at various points in my life.

Thus my path seemed to be destined for me as a spaceholder in my lineage, one who would continue where my ancestors left off. I have spent many years, through both traditional academic settings and mystical encounters, trying to understand the dynamics of good and evil in both this world and beyond the veil. What I have come to realize is the ability for me to hold space in any realm affords me the blessing of Presence, the blessing of the Divine. Holding space has become a discipline for me and for my writing. And that is what I hope to achieve when you read my words—the ability to hold space in both the darkness and the light for us to heal individually and collectively.

LIGHT CALLING FROM THE ABYSS

"Come a little closer," the darkness said, "I want to see your light."

"What is there to see?" I quivered.

The darkness looked bemused and took a step back as to not frighten me so. "Your perceptions of me are unfounded, rooted amidst desperation in trying to understand who you are.

You are as much afraid of me as you are of your light. Those heavy emotions that permeate your soul when left to despair, powerlessness, and hatred make me out to be something that I am not. I don't fuel those emotions within you. You do. You give those emotions power over you and then project blame onto me. And all I want to do is simply help you understand the balance between your light and me. And in order to do that, I need to get closer to you. Sometimes that may not be so comfortable, for both of us. As afraid of me as you are, I find myself a little frightened of your light too."

Seeing how vulnerable darkness was becoming, I walked closer to it, more curious of its nature. "How could you be afraid of my light? Look at all the harm you have perpetuated throughout humanity."

1

"I didn't cause humanity to suffer. Humans and their interpretations of me, their ability to choose—that is what caused their suffering.

"I have been and always will be a silent partner in the midst of Creation, only ignited by what humans fear most and acted upon by misguided thoughts.

"From the moment your soul felt abandoned by the Divine, you conjured up a manifestation of me to fill that void. My voice wasn't mine anymore. It became some construct of the collective used to further separate you from yourself, humanity from its collective soul.

"I search the universe, haunted by humanity's need to make me something I am not.

"I yearn to be that silent partner again in the midst of Creation. To stand by your side, holding hands with your light, understanding it as much as I want to understand myself."

I paused for a moment and then extended my hand.

Darkness, even more humbled by my offering, reached for it and came closer to me.

"I'd like to get to know you better," I said.

"I'd like that too." The darkness smiled.

As we held hands, our fears slowly began melting away, and the nature of the universe felt like home again.

◆ ◆ ◆

The one thing I am constantly reminded of by the spirit world is that grace never leaves your side. In those darkest of moments, when every perceived reality in your experience only reinforces a loneliness that brushes incessantly upon your soul, we can choose to remember the sacred silence we are birthed from. Portal to portal, heaven to womb, womb to earth, earth to dust,

dust to resurrection. Grace is the nectar that carries you between realms, from those in the ethers to the internal landscaping from which your thoughts and emotions flow. I know this year has been incredibly challenging for many. Grace soothes the chaos and calls it back home to God so that it may be held in Divine Providence, lessening its blow so that in its mercy, the chaos softens. And within its softening, we can be molded by the light. May you all feel the light of grace surround you.

◆ ◆ ◆

Every time the moon revolves around the sun, it whispers sweet nothings into her ears. If only humans did the same with one another.

◆ ◆ ◆

You are stronger than your wound.

◆ ◆ ◆

You are birthed from both light and darkness.

From the wombs of your mother and her mother before her.

From the sins of your past and those of your lineage.

From the sacredness that has enveloped your soul and carried you though every incarnation.

You are birthed from the rawness of innocence and the darkest of mysteries.

From the unbridled rage that permeates collective generations

To the forgiveness that ambles gently behind it.

From the angels that hear your fervent prayers

To the demons that abscond with them.

You are birthed neither male nor female,

But of flesh, bone and blood,

To which you have ascribed an identity that pulls you away from that which you truly are—

A fertile energy from source, emanating polarities of universal threads,

Encompassing good and evil.

One day, you will come to accept all that you are.

♦ ♦ ♦

When you stand at the threshold of loss, there will be this inexplicable force pulling you into the abyss of night, compelling you to fall deeper into the unknown.

Where emotions run rampant until overwhelm takes hold of every sense of your being, rendering a feeling of powerlessness amidst every facet of your identity.

You wait, with trepidation, until you feel twinges of anything recognizable that makes you feel somewhat human again.

This loss, so destabilizing, so unavoidable, empties you into nothingness like no other you have ever encountered.

Unable to be remedied by human understanding, this loss needs the one thing to make the unknown somewhat gentler for you, somewhat less terrifying.

It needs grace.

When you stand at the threshold, may you allow grace to walk before you, beside you, around you and within you.

May it compel the powerlessness that you feel to see the light calling to you from the abyss, shedding any remnants of a past identity so that a new identity may rise from the ashes.

May it shelter your humanity so that what you perceive outside of yourself is fleeting, allowing loss to become part of the whole, part of the light without your losing yourself amidst the darkness.

◆ ◆ ◆

I find that once people become familiar with their own darkness, they find it hard to let it go. At times, it provides them with a sense of empowerment and safety they have not known before. Embracing the Light can be a more frightening experience. When held in the threshold of the Divine, any darkness can serve a higher purpose, as it allows one to return to the Light if one is willing to surrender and learn from it. My prayer is that we all create a space for the darkness to birth a new way of seeing, sensing, feeling and relating. May our darkness find the balance it needs to serve humanity as opposed to igniting chaos. May we stop projecting our sense of powerlessness and feeding that place inside of us that feels bound to a reality that we continually create with our fears. May we respect the teachings of the Masters within us, our thoughts and emotions, with a humility that births Creation and not destruction. Darkness can perpetually serve the darkness, or it can evolve to serve the Light of God. Which path do you choose?

◆ ◆ ◆

I remember the day I asked God a question.

I was waiting for Her usual reply of yes or no, but instead She whispered into my ear, "I don't know."

Her response sent me spiraling into myself, into the unknown, into a world of possibilities amidst every realm imaginable.

I began to resent Her. More so, I began to resent myself.

Then I paused for a moment, a long moment.

I took a deep breath and realized that was the greatest gift I ever received.

"I don't know" opened up doors to such sacred places inside

my heart and mind that I burst with enormous tears of joy at the immense sense of empowerment those few words brought to my soul.

♦ ♦ ♦

There are moments I choose to see limitations as God's way of setting a boundary for us that we aren't aware we need at the time.

♦ ♦ ♦

You are not feeling threatened by life. You are feeling threatened by the unknown. There is a difference.

♦ ♦ ♦

I don't see this as the end of the world. I see this as the end of old ways and patterns—patterns that governed our archaic ways of thinking, loving, experiencing, forgiving, and just being. I see this as a time of expansion beyond what we deem is humanity toward a more sacred existence that infuses our relationship with each other with more grace than we could ever have imagined.

♦ ♦ ♦

Don't shelter me from the storm.
Instead, teach me to be still
As it quivers amidst my strength.

♦ ♦ ♦

I trembled my entire life until I felt that tabernacle of holiness had never left me, leaving me with a semblance of self I never thought would exist only, to find a constant companion in the eternal quest within.

◆ ◆ ◆

The sun never realized the light of its own being until it paused one day to see all that had blossomed in its path.

◆ ◆ ◆

The earth is helping us to understand the difference between entitlement and humility. The virus itself is also learning the same lessons.

The energies being created through this virus will ground themselves into the genetic matrices of both humans and the earth alike. Years down the road, our bodies will have learned lessons they needed to learn to be in relationship with what we perceive now as a threat to our humanity.

I wonder if the virus feels as threatened as we do with its possible eradication. A living and "breathing" intelligence is working to understand its role in the universe, its own relationship to humanity, and its relationship to its own survival.

Entitlement and humility, a balance, one day, perhaps.

◆ ◆ ◆

"Follow me," the darkness said.

"Why?" I quivered.

"Maybe I'm what you need to remember your light. There are easier ways, but your nature is curious and your inadequacy great."

I pondered for a moment.

"Will I truly remember?"

"It's up to you. But once you remember, I will not look the same anymore."

"Why not?"

"You will no longer have the need to see me in the same

way. To explore me with the same mind, to listen to me with the same heart. I will not be something you fear, but a constant companion, ready to remind you that I too was once light. But I lost my way. I chose another path. I seek you out to remind you of what I once was. You seek me out to forget who you truly are. We need each other. We always will."

◆ ◆ ◆

There are days I want to be a solitary raindrop amidst the impending storm, whose power and might lie within its intrepid stillness.

◆ ◆ ◆

Your path has been witnessed already
By those who have met God.
Honor the unknown.

◆ ◆ ◆

Your life needs you.

◆ ◆ ◆

An act of mercy can humble any darkness.

◆ ◆ ◆

Piece by piece, you gather yourself gently until your life story becomes one that you are no longer afraid to tell.

◆ ◆ ◆

We may not always get the chance to write our own story, but we have the power to choose how to tell it.

◆ ◆ ◆

There will come a time when you lose interest in telling your story from that familiar wounded place. You will lose interest in those perceptions that keep you shackled from living an authentic life. You will lose interest in repeating words that dampen your spirit and continue to hold you accountable for pain that no longer serves you.

There will come a time when your spirit wants to soar with reckless abandon in the creation of a new story. The images might be the same; the words might be familiar. The wound will still be present. Your story will become more powerful than the wound because you have finally allowed it to be. The images and words will finally be given the space to find sanctity so that your story is not only birthed anew but made holy for all eternity.

◆ ◆ ◆

Inspired by a true story.
You.
Yes, you.
A love so luminous you burst forth into Creation,
And every star in the galaxy wept with tears of joy.

◆ ◆ ◆

A story once told is never forgotten.

Even when the mind forgets, the wind remembers, the stars reminisce, the moon smiles, and the heavens share your story with all Creation.

Be at ease with what you think is lost, for all your memories are held by the holiest of friends above.

Your story will always be sacred.

◆ ◆ ◆

Your footprints will tell the truth of your story long after you are gone, even when the words you speak in this lifetime cannot.

♦ ♦ ♦

If you can't change your story, change how you see yourself in it.

♦ ♦ ♦

The splendor of your innocence was never lost. It was simply forgotten. You were afraid to remember. Frightened of the perceptions of any darkness that scorched your memory of an innocence so Divine. Remember it again. Run to it. The splendor awaits your return to an infinite wisdom that never left you.

♦ ♦ ♦

There is such beauty in the darkness, if you only knew where to look.

♦ ♦ ♦

There are times I don't want the storm to pass too quickly. I yearn to feel its waves fall upon my flesh, humbling every thought and emotion within me that compels me to hold on, molding me into an emptiness I have never known before, only to have me rise with a profound sense of awakening, a fierce knowing of inner strength, an intrepid love of self. Yes, I am here, waiting for you.

♦ ♦ ♦

Don't try to brave the storm all at once. One raindrop at a time. It will still heal you at depths unimaginable.

♦ ♦ ♦

Courage comes from creating a healing relationship between you and your fear.

♦ ♦ ♦

Our need for holiness becomes stronger each time we come face-to-face with our emptiness.

◆ ◆ ◆

The emptiness requires no effort to reach. Avoiding it will leave your soul in the darkness.

◆ ◆ ◆

The greatest obstacle you will ever encounter in this world is yourself.

◆ ◆ ◆

Anger untouched can lose itself amidst the need to justify a sense of powerlessness it has never understood.

It is an emotion that, when forged with fear at the very thought of its exploration, creates an identity around power even before we have a chance to identify it in its simplicity. Every emotion, in its raw state, has an innate and acquired innocence and offers us the opportunity to create spiritual and psychological boundaries toward evolutionary growth.

Do not be afraid of your anger.

You are more afraid of who you are in relationship to it than the emotion itself.

◆ ◆ ◆

Anger is not usually defined spiritually as a constructive emotion. Anger is an energy first and foremost. It is a fire energy that can either rise up from the earth element and evolve as it reaches the crown chakra or descend from the mind and distort itself as it reaches manifestation. It can also descend from the lower realms of the spirit world for those souls who are still working on their ancestral issues. It can attach to individuals and collectively to peoples as we all struggle to understand an emotion that has been a defining force for centuries when it comes to understanding one's own power.

That same fire energy that yields anger also births forgiveness, creativity, boundaries, purpose. Many on a spiritual path are uncomfortable with this energy and try to work through it faster than appropriate for their higher good. There is a time and place for every emotion, both in human and spiritual realms. Working through an emotion faster does not give rise to the healing relationship with it that most people desire. Actually, some would rather not have any relationship with anger at all. The idea of it can be overwhelming, confusing, debilitating. For others, it can be empowering, even uplifting. It all depends on one's relationship to it in alignment with the appropriate response that fulfills that soul's purpose. An appropriate response? Purpose? Yes, even in the higher realms, anger serves a purpose, but the intent is not the same. It is simply an energy that serves to direct reasoning, Providence, and forgiveness. In human realms, in order for us to learn that it is an energy to work with and respect, we have to work through the living experiences that our anger takes us to in order to rise above. We are all given a choice as to how to carry the anger, relate to it, manifest it, and direct it. This fire energy is incredibly strong right now, and I believe Divine Providence is providing us with the awareness to carry it with a new understanding, which is why I am noticing people are being so easily triggered these days. Avoiding the fire will only make the flames more powerful. Standing at its threshold, honoring its power and purpose, deciding in stillness what course of action to take—that will transmute this emotion into the energy it was meant to be.

♦ ♦ ♦

Don't deny anger when it arrives at your doorstep. Rather, treat it with the innocence of a newborn baby, whose purity of mind and heart would identify with that emotion in a much gentler and simpler way. Your anger will then have a greater opportunity to transform itself instead of being used to fill a void that, when unveiled, is part of your inner holy ground. The only way to witness this is to walk the path.

You become your path the moment you set foot on the ground. Whether or not you chose that direction doesn't matter anymore.

It is where you are now.

Become the teacher.

Become the student.

Become the partner.

Become the relationship you always wanted to have with yourself.

♦ ♦ ♦

Love is a word that can often be misused and misinterpreted when it comes to being in relationship. We enter into relationship to help us understand the duality of our natures and, effectually, to understand more about the human and spiritual condition. We are drawn to various people because of energetic conditioning; and how one's psyche interprets that conditioning depends on the human and spiritual needs and lessons at that moment in time. Love seems like a simplistic notion, yet most of us find it challenging to rise about our psychological constraints to love well. After all, loving well is one of the most challenging tasks at hand for many of us.

Our interpretations have to work through years of psychological patterning; ancestral miasms; and societal, cultural, and world paradigms. In loving well, we are faced with a surrender of self to such a degree that it triggers our deepest fears around self-sacrifice and abandonment. Some of us might equate that with suffering. Establishing safe zones for us to explore in relationship further enhances the notion that in order to love well, we need to relinquish our attachment to ego in order to fulfill an inconceivable destiny. Why inconceivable? The losses incurred as a part of emotional evolution during the process of loving well can seem overpowering and overwhelming, enabling us to place conditions on our partners and ourselves in this dance of relationship. How many of us are afraid to approach the inner work encouraged to explore a love like this? Many of us.

When we define or attach our suffering to love, we have already identified our self-worth and the love our partner may have for us within the same paradigm. In this manner, love becomes an internal power struggle between the ego and the higher self, between the heart and the mind, between one's sense of powerlessness and one's authentic nature. Our fear will continue to draw in more experiences to help further this notion.

♦ ♦ ♦

Some are running fast toward enlightenment to escape the pain, the emptiness of being.

♦ ♦ ♦

God doesn't falter. He/She takes a step back until the illusion we've created no longer serves the purpose we think it serves. This confusion over free will versus Divine Will—it's not the heavens who remain confounded, but we who continue to hold on to the illusion.

♦ ♦ ♦

In the midst of this worldwide crisis, you are feeling everything unimaginable to the very core of your being.

You are being stripped of familiar boundaries in every relationship you have with yourself and with others.

◆ ◆ ◆

In the abyss of humanity, the depravity on which a mind and heart can churn reality when faced with such isolation of self can be overwhelming.

So is what one craves in order to extinguish a darkness it seemingly has no power over, even when approached by the light.

It may not recognize the light, for fear of embracing those aspects of self that yearn to be touched so deeply that any form of solace feels threatening.

The darkness calls to you as much as the light.

"Touch me," it says.

"Touch me deeply so I may know you; so I may know myself."

You are so used to running from it, you become that which you fear most.

The unknown.

The unknown and the abyss are not the same, but you covet such freedom from what torments you that you cannot see clearly.

The emptiness fills you until you become hollow.

The darkness isn't asking this of you.

Your mind is.

The darkness is asking to play with your light. To seek shelter in your holiness.

A holiness that you have been afraid to touch the moment you shut down and saw yourself as an intrinsic part of the abyss, unable to breathe light into your own being and that of the world.

Time to wake up, children of God; the light of the unknown awaits you.

◆ ◆ ◆

Bind me with your judgment and I will retaliate with my own sense of self. It will be more powerful and empowering than any unhealed version you dreamed up because *you* were the one afraid to shine.

◆ ◆ ◆

The night will always appear laden in darkness until you actually allow yourself to see the stars.

◆ ◆ ◆

The strength to keep going never left you. You were simply afraid of just how strong you actually were.

◆ ◆ ◆

We are only as broken as we think we are.

◆ ◆ ◆

The more frightened you are of your darkness, the greater the power it has over you.

◆ ◆ ◆

Oh, tormented earth, forgive us our trespasses as we have forgotten our own sacredness amidst your gentle womb. We walk upon your flesh, indignant in our right to take from you what does not belong to us. We have forgotten that in all that we are, you provide the sustenance of our living breath, the nourishment of our beating hearts, the wisdom of our compromised minds. May we endeavor to know you completely and uninhibited by a fear so powerful that it diminishes our capacity to respect you in ways you deserve to be respected. Oh, Mother Earth, forgive us our trespasses. We know what we are doing wrong. May we be given the courage to rise and do what needs to be done.

♦ ♦ ♦

There is an order to chaos that is so distinctly sublime in the eyes of the Divine. Touch upon it so that your own inner chaos may meet mercy at the threshold of a new understanding.

There is an order to chaos so distinctly sublime in the eyes of the Creator. An order that the ego cannot comprehend in its usual state of wounded manifestation. There is a time for that chaos to be impinged upon by human interaction, and a time for it to unwind into destiny guided by the Laws of Providence. When left to be touched by the hand of God, chaos has a way of finding the light faster than if left to the interference and interpretation of humankind.

♦ ♦ ♦

Surrender to the profound in those places within you that frighten you so.

♦ ♦ ♦

May we all return home to that inner sanctuary infused with a grace so Divine, so unblemished, that Presence becomes our only desire.

♦ ♦ ♦

The greatest distance between you and your Beloved is your mind.

♦ ♦ ♦

God quieted me in what I thought was stillness when He whispered into my soul. Only then could I truly comprehend the vastness of all that I was meant to be. Only then could I embrace a stillness that no human mind could understand until I released myself, without fear, into the unknown, waiting to be molded into a form that only the stillness could define.

Many of us who do '"the work" also use the work as an escape mechanism. We bargain to keep some sort of control over those parts of us that are yearning to be let go of. We become trapped in our internal chaos, trying to find the stillness without the suffering one will go through in order to love well. Nobody wants to struggle, yet it seems to be an integral part of life. We can learn to allow for the struggle to humble us in such a way that it also empowers us with the wisdom and graces of the Divine. If we do, we no longer feel trapped inside of ourselves, as the fear of loving is lessened. This is the struggle we go through to receive such a powerful blessing and experience. If only our interpretations and attachments would not render us helpless. That's not love's intentions. That is fear.

In loving well, we engage in the present. Many times, we circle back to various realities to fulfill an undefined version that only continues to fuel the fear. We will seek to not suffer and spend a great part of our lives working effortlessly to achieve that space. The energy expended only causes us more, and sometimes it will involve us further into those dark places where we don't need to go. All the while, both you and your partner are waiting to give and receive a love that you are both destined for.

Relationships were not meant to be easy. They were meant to challenge our inner realities and the paradigms we have created to keep us safe emotionally. In loving well, we most certainly will be stepping out of our comfort zone. But that's a chance I'm willing to take if it means a life of living and loving well.

◆ ◆ ◆

Faith can spread like wildfire in the most vulnerable of spaces, leaving you destined to follow the path of your heart and not the misgivings of your mind.

♦ ♦ ♦

May our inadequacies be gently humbled into a state of pure bliss that can only be ignited by the Divine.

♦ ♦ ♦

There are moments God leaves me breathless. Whether in the light or in the darkness, I need a tender moment to gather and find myself again.

♦ ♦ ♦

We see things differently once we experience loss.
We live life differently once we heal from it.

♦ ♦ ♦

There is this place, this middle ground inside of ourselves that teeters on the brink of darkness, grasping at strings of light when raw with emotion. The darkness appears vast and the light seems unreachable. Telling ourselves we will be okay seems fruitless, an escape from presence. Ensconced in shame, the word "okay" has taken on such an identity when it comes to how we are feeling.

I found myself sharing in sessions this week that it was okay NOT to be okay. Many people I spoke with were deluged with emotional crises, fear rising as the thought of not being okay equated with survival on many levels—survival of identity and roles in this world and within their familial and work environment; survival of their hearts, their minds, their physical bodies. When loved ones would ask them how they were doing, the ensuing response of "I'm okay" just wasn't adequate enough. Adequate in their minds in regard to themselves, but in truth, the recipient hearing those words may not know how to respond to someone saying that they are not okay. Being not okay and owning it can trigger a sense of powerlessness, weakness, inadequacy, and shame. It is as though it is not okay to not feel okay. We might share those feelings with those closest to us and hide it with the rest of the world, where I bet most of us equate experiences of not being okay with not feeling okay.

I remember the silence on the other end of the phone this week in a few sessions. When I shared that it was completely okay not to be okay, it was like opening a door to the underworld. There was a space created to forgive the self-judgment and allow for a sense of empowerment to be felt when truth rings authentic. There was a space created so the internal power struggle could quiet itself and find breathing room to expand its thoughts and emotions. A space where weakness, inadequacy, and shame didn't make sense anymore, as not being okay suddenly became powerfully okay.

◆ ◆ ◆

Once I stepped into the abyss, I realized I wasn't the same person I used to be a moment ago. I would become a different person with each step I took moving forward. If only I could see in me what the abyss already knew. How could I, when I judged it as being separate from myself? The abyss is not what we are afraid of. We are frightened of who we think we are in a perceived reality where every construct we have created to define ourselves is within our grasp. Our constructs of self-preservation have only made us more intimidated by our true selves than by any unknown darkness or emptiness we might ever encounter.

◆ ◆ ◆

The precipice is only as steep as you envision it. The precipice itself is not daunting. Your fear of it is.

♦ ♦ ♦

There is this place in the house of the gods where your grief and the grief of your ancestors can return to its truest nature, its purest form. There is this place where forgiveness dwells amidst the wings of angels, where tears become rooted in a strength so profound that eternal peace is thrust into Creation by the very sacredness sourced from that grief. As you enter into that sacredness, the gods rejoice.

♦ ♦ ♦

Emerge out of chaos to find gentleness awaiting you, enough so that you are comforted amidst your transformation.

♦ ♦ ♦

In the presence of holiness, anything that is created that does not serve your highest good can be uncreated.

♦ ♦ ♦

You will eventually return to self. That is the path. The ebb and flow of the Divine within you compels you to go deeper into your humanity to remember your own sacred Creation. How can you not be sacred? Touch that holiness. It will be the light on your path that you never saw coming.

♦ ♦ ♦

I give thanks to the moon for echoing my prayers.

I bow my head before the sun for delivering my words to the heavens.

The winds harken to the sounds of my yearning for the Creator.

The trees dance with merriment as I await an answer.

The earth embraces my form in a humbled stance.

Creation moves effortlessly between those prayers from the earth to the heavens.

The answer serves not only me, but all of Creation.

If my prayer honored just one, the earth would weep.

Before my prayer is received by the gods, it is held by those living manifestations in the natural world.

If I were to not recognize the moon, the sun, the winds, the trees, any of God's creations brought forth to accompany us on this journey, then my prayer is not really a prayer at all.

May I never forget to honor you, Oh gentle earth, whose soul is righteous, whose prayer is more powerful than we human beings could ever imagine.

Your inner peace avails itself differently from someone else's. Trying to diminish another's understanding of Presence only diminishes your own.

♦ ♦ ♦

Eventually, every darkness gets tired of running away from the light.

♦ ♦ ♦

I will meet you all at the edge of the abyss—where the darkness meets the light in holy union, surrendering, one wound at a time.

♦ ♦ ♦

We are being awakened from the longest sleep in human history. God just put on Her dancing shoes. Are you ready to come alive again?

♦ ♦ ♦

The stillness within a storm renders me powerless against a Will that is greater than my own contrived human understanding. How I long in such times to be reminded that humility is an opportunity to be carried by the silence of Creation.

◆ ◆ ◆

In times of desperation, there is a softening we can let seep into our hearts; one that confronts our fears mercifully. A softening that invites a gentle compassion, a womb-like trance dancing amidst faith as it ebbs and flows from the Divine into our own physical beings, reaching into the depths of the earth while soaring between the heavenly realms.

A softening that is not afraid of the desperation, instead offering shelter, an abode that carries the darkness as gracefully as it carries the light.

◆ ◆ ◆

Birth yourself slowly unto this new world,

Reaching toward the heavens one star at a time

While rooting yourself amidst earthen creatures awaiting your gentle friendship.

Behold such beauty in the breath of Creation, where you will be woven into a story you do not know yet.

A story so emblazoned with light that angels weep

At the sight of your evolution,

At the sight of you being rebirthed as the prayer you were meant to be for all humanity.

◆ ◆ ◆

When I asked God to show me the path, She held up a mirror, and for the very first time I saw myself. Then when I screamed at God at how powerless I felt, She extended her hand and showed me the universe.

◆ ◆ ◆

If only we remembered how gently to carry ourselves, as God has carried us in Her womb.

◆ ◆ ◆

It's beginning to thunder outside my home.

I've been waiting all day for this meeting of realms, this elevation of souls.

My body heavily laden with density today of a different vibration.

A vibration whose tears are sculpted in grief of those who have yet to pass in physical form but whose spirits have already been taken upon wings of angels.

Many times I bear witness to those who are to cross soon, as they pass through me, above me, and beyond me,

Letting me know a significant exodus will occur in some reality of our molded experience,

Humbled to be a part of the alleviation of the suffering of the collective,

Awakening to the unknown within the tabernacle of the gods.

All of us have moved into this dimension now,

Serving the collective transformation of a power misguided into the depths of humility humankind has not seen before.

I can hear the rain now, the most beautiful rain

Reaching into the corners of my heart, softening the edges hardened by incarnations past,

Soothing tenderness, bound by a love humanity will soon experience of such profundity.

Mind your soul in this splendid moment—

The changes subtle yet awe inspiring.

◆ ◆ ◆

The powerless will rise and see that their voices were always heard. Not by the ignorant ears of humans, but by the majestic souls beyond the veil whose prayers fall upon God's ears.

◆ ◆ ◆

Nourish yourself beyond any comprehension you think you have attained about self-love. Your heart's capacity to receive love is not something that can be taught, but achieved through the experience of grace revealed

In increments of tenderness like droplets of dew on a blossoming flower,

Caressing each petal in harmony with heaven's symphony

Only to show you just how much you are truly wanted

So that the experience of loving yourself becomes nothing less than utter bliss.

◆ ◆ ◆

As a response to trauma, it is much easier at times for us to become hypnotized and sensitized to power that embeds itself in darkness than to a power that is beholden to the light.

Our understanding and expression through crisis dismantles our very being to the core, and an intrinsic reaction is to feel as empowered as we can to protect ourselves, not seeing clearly where the power is coming from. Until we create healthier systemic relationships to trauma both individually and collectively, our relationship to power itself might always be skewed.

◆ ◆ ◆

On the edge of chaos,
I stood there waiting for you—
The self your dreams are made of,

Unencumbered by your past,
A new beginning to an end that never was.
I never left you.
It is you who left me.
In fear of who you were.
In fear of who I am.
Living on the edge only seeing the abyss,
ensconced within your deepest fears
Until I grabbed your hand,
But only because you let me.
I knew then that you were ready
To see the chaos differently,
To see yourself differently.
I paused a moment and then called you by your name.
You answered and set your gaze upon the heavens. My, how
lovely a name you have.
You smiled and then asked me mine.
"Grace," I answered.
"You can call me Grace."

◆ ◆ ◆

A whole new world within you awaits.

◆ ◆ ◆

You can't uncreate love.
You can uncreate the ways in which you love,
how much you love,
the choices you make on whom to love,
your thoughts on love,
and how much energy you choose to expend on trusting love.
I'd rather just love.
All the other stuff is too time consuming.

◆ ◆ ◆

What was once hallowed ground will be once again, simply because we will all come to understand holiness in ways we have not experienced before. The spirits were dancing today in my prayers as we have crossed yet another threshold, with the energies feeling a little lighter today, a respite from the heaviness for a moment in earthly time yet encompassing many parallel realities beyond the veil. Many of you might feel "different," unlike your "old" self. That is because you are different, and you will continue to rebuild a genetic and soul matrix influenced by the convergence of these parallel realities.

◆ ◆ ◆

When the mountain seems too difficult to climb, some choose to change their path. I choose to change my shoes.

2

FORGIVENESS

Forgiveness is both an act and a way of being. It is a process by which we take the light of God and hold it with the intention that grace will nurture both the light and the darkness within. We take the suffering we experience in our lives and become more accepting of it as a pathway to peace, releasing old identities and forging Creation both internally and externally as we rebirth ourselves. It is the process of being, the essence of being, and the essence of grace within that state of being. Forgiveness is not just something you practice. It becomes you.

◆ ◆ ◆

There comes a time when you simply cannot hold space for another in the way that you used to. Perhaps you changed. Or perhaps the space you held changed and you just didn't notice because you were holding on so tightly.

◆ ◆ ◆

I wish for a world where we spend more time seeking the good in others.

◆ ◆ ◆

In all my years of training, I never cared about being enlightened. I cared about being kind.

◆ ◆ ◆

Create a healthier relationship to your desperation before it becomes the motivating force for your life during these times.

◆ ◆ ◆

Since I was a child, I remember in a past life being burned at the stake for my healing medicine. I told the naysayers, "Go ahead. I will rise from my ashes and be more powerful than you could ever imagine, as forgiveness will be my greatest strength while hatred will be your greatest weakness."

◆ ◆ ◆

The deepest grief you will ever know is when you cannot forgive those who hurt you. And the greatest loss you will ever encounter is when you cannot forgive yourself.

◆ ◆ ◆

The moment you have to prove yourself worthy is the moment you really don't know who you actually are.

◆ ◆ ◆

Sometimes when we fall short of forgiveness we become too comfortable with the bitterness we keep.

◆ ◆ ◆

A power struggle exists between two people when they fall prey to the illusion that they both have something inherent to lose.

◆ ◆ ◆

Be that person who forgives long before the apology ever happens.

◆ ◆ ◆

Grace is afforded to every child of God, but many times it is the humble who are willing to recognize its splendor.

◆ ◆ ◆

The measure of a true human being is someone who extols the worthiness in others so that he may eventually see it within himself.

◆ ◆ ◆

Step into your own identity without having to tear someone else's apart.

◆ ◆ ◆

Extend a hand and you extend your heart. Extend your heart and you will extend a life.

◆ ◆ ◆

Bear witness to your own humility, or lack thereof, before contemplating another's. You will see things more clearly.

◆ ◆ ◆

You don't need to extinguish someone else's flame so that your own fire may burn brightly.

◆ ◆ ◆

It is not the silence you fear. It is who you perceive yourself to be in the midst of it.

The moment you think you have "worked through it all," the silence will no longer be silent.

It will arise with uncertainty and ask the questions you have been afraid to answer.

The questions that erupt into a cycle of isolation, spiraling heart and mind into oblivion, creating chaos that longs to be justified.

The silence needs nothing from you.

It is you who need its tenderness amidst the chaos, its comfort amidst the grief, its grace amidst the confusion.

❖ ❖ ❖

The silence never left you.
You escaped from it much of your life,
wandering through deserts in search of yourself.
Only to return to the same place you started from.
My, how long a journey you made,
in struggling more than you needed to.

One day you will meet fear face-to-face, and it will challenge your every inhibition. Then the day will come when you
will meet fear heart-to-heart, and it will ask your every forgiveness for its trespasses upon you.

❖ ❖ ❖

Wounds heal all time
The past, the present, the future
If you allow them to.

❖ ❖ ❖

Every element in nature has opposing realities, as does every element within the spirit world. I also view the human body and
how we nourish it with the same perspective.

When I work with a person who comes to me to find the
origin of his or her ailments or, many times, to even diagnose to
the level I am capable of, I first ask a few questions. I venture into
the spirit world to look at the patterning of both parents and
at the patterns that continue to be worked on beyond the veil, as
well as the tissues and cellular level of the person I am working
with. Just as DNA is passed on, so is cellular memory, energetic
memory, and spiritual miasms. Illness is caused and triggered by
many factors, not just one. I have to take into account what factors are holding strongest to the pattern, identify them, and see
how we can best balance them.

One of the stories I share in my classes involves a woman I assisted over twenty years ago. She came to me with fibromyalgia and Chronic Fatigue Immune Dysfunction. The moment she walked in, I saw the shackles around her wrists and ankles and an ancestral spirit standing behind her. I knew immediately that whatever she would present with, there was a strong spiritual and ancestral miasm influencing her health. In her tissues, her ailments were clearly confirmed by her pulses and the way I noticed her fascia shifting upon palpation. All ailments have a vibration, just like anything else. It became second nature to be able to discern various ailments and even medications still in the body upon palpating. We have a relationship with everything we put into our bodies, every ailment that we face, every emotion we feel and every thought we create. I even suggest remedies that our bodies are able to create a healing relationship with. As with my client, I had to suggest remedies that both her body and the ancestral spirit holding the pattern standing behind her would accept. This was about more than just her body being healed, but a long-standing familial dynamic that needed some attention. Little by little, as relationships take time, things began to shift for her. As the spirit shifted, what her body needed shifted as well and vice versa. We worked for a while and then parted ways. We were able to get to a certain place, but I knew the spirit needed more time to heal as did her body, and she was exhausted from doing so much work on herself. Understandably so.

When the time was right, we crossed paths again. The moment I saw her I looked for those shackles. I did not see them. I also did not see the ancestral spirit lingering anymore. He had crossed into the light. I asked her how she was feeling physically, and she no longer felt those ailments that had been plaguing her. Her tissues were much better upon palpation and overall, she had a part of her life back that she felt she had lost.

Not everyone's ailments are influenced in that way to that extent. Some are indeed influenced by trauma, environmental factors, and familial dynamics, but I will always look for the ancestral DNA first to see what miasms are inherited so I know what I am working with. Looking at the human body from a multidimensional perspective is key to healing.

◆ ◆ ◆

The raw beauty of nature embraces its ability to surrender to the gods to serve all of Creation. It does not falter when asked to accept a higher will that will serve a purpose unbeknownst to it at times. It understands that even with death, the beauty lives on as an imprint to show humankind the goodness that we are all capable of.

◆ ◆ ◆

No one is without grace. Lose sight of it in others and you just made your own journey that much more difficult.

◆ ◆ ◆

Practice forgiveness until you no longer seek it outside of yourself.

◆ ◆ ◆

Your peace of mind has to do with the way you live your life, not the way others live theirs.

◆ ◆ ◆

Don't silence another person's voice because you're afraid of using your own.

◆ ◆ ◆

Every person's relationship to suffering looks different on the outside. Be kind.

◆ ◆ ◆

Through parallel realities, may the love we have for life reach into the fabric of the universe and touch upon our ancestors who brought us here. May that love foster a forgiveness so unencumbered that our ancestors rejoice with pride. I pray that we remember a mercy so profound it sends ripples through all of Creation. May we continue to unfold into sacredness, embraced by an energy that births light upon light.

◆ ◆ ◆

A smile can be so extraordinarily powerful when offered to someone who thinks he or she is unworthy of it.

◆ ◆ ◆

Forgive without fear and the path to self-acceptance will be much gentler.

◆ ◆ ◆

An ordinary life sometimes requires extraordinary measures when it comes to practicing forgiveness.

◆ ◆ ◆

A person's story goes beyond their words. Deny their story and on some level you deny your own.

◆ ◆ ◆

Become invincible. Love with such a humility that even the angels bow before you.

◆ ◆ ◆

There are days I wake up waiting to be captivated by God and all Her creations.

♦ ♦ ♦

We were born from the earth as much as we were born from the gods. Respect both worlds.

♦ ♦ ♦

May your spirits be humbled by a love so powerful. May your hearts be comforted by a presence so Divine. May your minds be graced by a forgiveness unparalleled. And may your journeys be held by a holiness unimaginable.

♦ ♦ ♦

No other traveler can understand your grief in the ways God intended for your journey. A solitary purpose ensconced in a collective dream woven of stories from hearts struggling with loss, despair, abandonment, and hopelessness. The doors to our original wounding in this lifetime, those scars made visible by both our humanity and Divinity, only lessened by brief moments of grace. The door between the past and the present makes us unsure of the landscape unfolding, watching as this next layer of grief unwinds itself into something unknown, something so vulnerable yet powerful in its evolution. Even if we have no understanding of its purpose at the present moment in time, may we respect it as a part of our sacred story.

♦ ♦ ♦

Such an extraordinary task we are each given, to love one another unconditionally.

Judging another person's response to his or her life story might just diminish the power and authenticity of your own.

♦ ♦ ♦

You are not stuck.

You are simply learning patience until God gives you the green light

That the runway is clear.

♦ ♦ ♦

I don't believe in shattered dreams.

I believe in shattered belief systems.

Dreams simply avail themselves differently amidst the time and space continuum when one's heart surrenders to faith and the power of Creation.

You are allowing a dream to become fulfilled by the hand of the Divine igniting it.

♦ ♦ ♦

Innocence is a gateway to trusting beyond a measurable doubt that you are completely and utterly loved.

♦ ♦ ♦

There is a distinct relationship between your usefulness in this world and how much you believe you are truly loved.

♦ ♦ ♦

As the prophet spoke with such eloquence, those who gained the most wisdom were the ones who heard the silence and not the actual words spoken.

♦ ♦ ♦

Pray deeply until you feel held.

Pray deeply until you feel heard.

Pray deeply until you feel healed.

Pray deeply until you feel comforted.

Pray deeply until you feel Him.

Pray deeply until you feel Her.

Pray deeply until you feel yourself.

✦ ✦ ✦

Sometimes the best place to find yourself is that place you feel most lost.

✦ ✦ ✦

Be fearless in your integrity so that others may rise with you.

✦ ✦ ✦

Those who fail to appreciate the gentle spirit of a tree may never recognize the light of his own heart.

✦ ✦ ✦

There are days when my conversations with trees yield a kindness that I hope to see one day amidst humans.

✦ ✦ ✦

Ritual is a sacred unfoldment where you enhance the possibilities between you and the Divine within the vast stillness of being, where the guiding force compels each one of us to break down the barriers between heaven and earth from the very core of our humanity to the highest dimension within the spirit world. As we return to self, each step we take invokes a communication between our lower and higher selves, between the individual and collective, and between parallel realities, including those who yearn for our acknowledgment beyond the veil. Enter into ritual reverently and you will enter into yourself reverently.

✦ ✦ ✦

There is somewhere inside of all of us that knows when a desire cannot be truly satiated. That fear alone perpetuates our search, our confusion, our turmoil. That fear alone perpetuates and emphasizes our need to be greater than it is in reality. But in being so caught up in the energy of addiction, we fail to see that the need is no longer a need but has taken on form. It becomes a power play—you against the energy, you against the fear, and ultimately, you against yourself.

With addiction, we set up a framework for our minds to protect and defend our inner landscape. The energy exchange between the person struggling with addiction and the object of the addiction creates a power vacuum—power not only feeding into one another, but in defense of one another, vying for control and understanding on some level. The use of power becomes self-destructive and self-validating in a distorted way, and it can become challenging for us to recognize and more importantly admit that we are hurting ourselves out of fear, pain, and the need for self-love.

Addictions do not serve reality; they serve illusion and will continue to do so as long as we hold on to them tightly. They will appear strong in might within the illusion. We need trust. There is a greater might within trust that will take us out of the illusion and into the light. We are as afraid of the energy behind the addiction as we are of letting go of it. The strength of the addiction is indicative of how strong our fear is as we work to let it go. What resists will persist and will gather strength. If it is illusion and not reality, it will gather strength in the illusion and perpetuate the cycle of darkness.

Some addictions need to leave our lives and complete a miasm that might have been in our lineage for generations, masking itself in various forms. Some might need to stay to complete an ancestral lesson. The miasm will serve in its capacity as it heals itself when we maintain awareness of our interactions, responses, and relationship with addiction.

So how does one recognize an addiction? We all have them in one way or another. Take a look at your lives. Look at a relational response that becomes repetitive, a misguided source of power that leaves you drained and within the emptiness, not believing there is light to be found. Ponder your relationship to it and notice if you identify it as harmful to you physically, emotionally, mentally, or spiritually. You can recognize an addiction by the intensity involved in the relationship to the object you are addicted to. By separating the object from what you think it is giving you and holding your fear around its absence, you can begin to source your true power. You have to place yourself in the center of the fear and the pain and see if you can withstand it gently in your heart. Within that space, your emptiness has great power within the light.

An addiction is not merely something we are drawn to. It becomes its own entity, and we have a relationship with it as though it were a friend, a child, a parent, a sibling. The relationship we create takes on a form that loses its authenticity in nature. The focus of the addiction no longer holds meaning in the way that it did before we developed a codependent relationship with it. Its meaning or intention changes itself as we dive deeper into its energies. The addiction changes form as we change with it. The relationship becomes more than it is in reality and more than it needs to be.

The miasm that propelled us into the addiction needs to be respected. There is healing medicine there. I don't believe it is us versus an addiction. Like all relationships, there is always something that serves a greater good, and the medicine we take when we take the energies behind the addiction into the light will be everlasting.

◆ ◆ ◆

It's time for Eve to embrace her power, Destiny be forever changed. The serpent only reminded her of her duality; her innocence lost in the confusion of self, in the Divine, in the world around her. The sacrifices of the feminine have shaped humanity, leaving teardrops at every threshold. Temptation challenged both her strengths and her weaknesses, until she became raw with emotion, searching for holiness in every crevice within herself.

Eve was brought to her knees not by the Divine, but by a paradise that was flawed in the very beginning of its inception, only to ignite shame in perceived wrongdoings of the soul. Reaching for forbidden fruit from the Tree of Knowledge is the beginning of one's inner work, shedding layers of self to eventually come to the understanding that true knowledge has no form. The nature of paradise is not to condemn. Eve knew that but questioned her own authenticity at the desire to know more, to feel more, to want more. There is no shame in human emotion, more so confusion. The projection of such emotion that arises out of desperation can inflict pain to self and to others. We are not descendants of original sin, but of a destiny of power emblazoned by love. The feminine is rising. Take heed of her strength. She will be the bearer of an extraordinary light and have the ability to bring darkness to its knees. The fruit of the Tree of Knowledge will be forbidden no more. In fact, Eve will forget it even existed as she sources from her own sacredness.

◆ ◆ ◆

Chaos has the power to become an extraordinary catalyst in surrendering to the Divine. Approach it reverently. Therein lies Providence, a sacred alignment humanity struggles with grasping in the face of the unknown. Never underestimate the light resting quietly within that chaos. You will find it once you meet surrender.

◆ ◆ ◆

Relish the unusual, as you never know when there might be angels in your midst.

When in haste, the path of least resistance might just be the unknown.

Tread lightly into another person's wounded space. Sacred territory abounds when wounds become collective in nature.

◆ ◆ ◆

The Tear

I sat there crying until I got to know my tears one by one.

Coming out into the world, a world amok with such disregard for human life, human love, tenderness, understanding, respect.

I could go on and on, but then more tears would come and my vessel that carries such raw emotion would want to retreat again.

Back to a time that most likely never existed in our human realm. A time where every tear shed was graced by a profound oneness existing only in dream time amidst angels.

To some people, you are the sunshine. To others, the filth beneath your feet scourged by a hatred unencumbered.

I sat there crying until I got to know my tears one by one.

Each one extraordinary as though God picked me a bouquet of flowers from Her garden.

Caressing my cheek as they strolled down with luminescent stories of each lifetime connected to them.

Those were the same tears my mother cried, my grandmother, and her mother before her.

The same tears my father shed, my grandfather, and his father before him.

The same tears my ancestors gently wiped from their weary visages.

The same tears that flowed from your face, your ancestors, your lineage.

My tears were greater in story than they appeared at first. In sitting with them, I got to know myself more deeply than I had ever known before.

More importantly, I got to know you. Each and every one of you.

I began to see you. Oh my, how you radiate with such immense beauty.

Every color of the rainbow, every voice of the ethers.

Every child created in the image and likeness of God.

Every child.

I think I will sit and cry again, so that I am able to hear more stories, stories about you, how precious you are to me, how loved you are despite the darkness that lurks in the shadows of ignorant minds.

I want to feel those tears until every story in Creation whispers their name into my ears with a voice so blessed by the heavens.

A voice that hasn't been heard yet in this realm but whose destiny is unfolding as human love is being sparked again by a consciousness that connects every tear ever cried in human history.

◆ ◆ ◆

Those who walk among us belong to the same tribe as those who walk within us. We are not separate.

◆ ◆ ◆

Meet me halfway and I will come to you running

With all the answers you will ever need.

In words unspoken, ignited by the explosion of love that cannot be contained in hearts alone.

With each breath I take, you will be my every beginning in this universe of light. Never broken or displaced by your love for me. Perhaps disheartened by your love for each other.

Meet me halfway and I will show you the love you are capable of. I would offer you the sun, the moon, and the stars, but you have them already. Born within you is a cornucopia of miracles, waiting for you to step into the light and receive.

◆ ◆ ◆

The ordinary within you has the potential to become the extraordinary when you allow little droplets of God to seep in.

◆ ◆ ◆

Honor the sacred within you before you lose yourself to that which is unholy. It is in those spaces that the Divine waits patiently to make your acquaintance.

◆ ◆ ◆

God's symphony played the music to your soul's imprint before you were even born. Every note put forth was in anticipation of your arrival through Her sacred portal; the womb that transformed those notes into the music that would teach you to dance for the rest of your life. Listen closely for your song. It will teach you everything you need to know about the dance.

◆ ◆ ◆

God doesn't open doors. She builds them large enough for us to see them on our paths. It is up to us to open them.

◆ ◆ ◆

You are never less than anyone else. Your worth is made holy by the same Power that brought you into this world.

◆ ◆ ◆

Our wounds are gateways to the light unimaginable.

◆ ◆ ◆

Hiding your wounds only makes them more visible. Respecting them makes you more peaceful.

◆ ◆ ◆

There are nights I dream of silence only to be awakened by the confusion of humankind—the chaos yearning to be healed by a love unparalleled in its experience. The illusion remains until night returns, and my dreams once more return me to an inner sanctuary where the silence becomes my refuge and my awakening.

◆ ◆ ◆

One day the sacred silence will be so ineffable, and its unspoken words will become the holiest to fall upon your ears.

◆ ◆ ◆

What matters are the words unspoken
Between the chaos and confusion of that which is deemed unholy.
Return to the portal that birthed you into existence
Into this experience of splendor personified
That which humanity has forgotten
A womb so sacred giving rise to all humankind, the feminine hand of God
Which does not need words amidst the chaos
Only love.

◆ ◆ ◆

Tender moments of grace infuse me like droplets of sunshine on a cloudy day.

◆ ◆ ◆

Bless your inner demons until their unworthiness remembers the light of their own being.

◆ ◆ ◆

Let your wounds become your life's prayer.
Once you do, you will never be the same person again.

◆ ◆ ◆

Grief has a way of grounding you further into yourself, in spaces you never knew existed inside your being. It has a way of settling into your bones and challenging your experience of living, loving, and letting go. Your relationship with grief will be one of the most influential relationships you will ever have in this lifetime. Carry it well.

◆ ◆ ◆

The dehumanization of other human beings begins at home. Tend to your own self-worth first.

◆ ◆ ◆

There are times God takes you gently by the hand. It might feel like a soft breeze whispering through your hair, letting you know over and over again just how much you are loved. Be open to Her touch, and you will never know loneliness again.

◆ ◆ ◆

Enter into a person's life reverently.
Your inner story will interact with theirs in ways unrecognized by your mind's limitations.

◆ ◆ ◆

You were born to bloom, especially on those days the sun doesn't shine.

◆ ◆ ◆

Transgenerational powerlessness—indoctrinated in every society, in every culture, in every mind.

The current state of the world is no different from historical accounts of war, devastation, famine, and abuses.

Emotional and psychological setbacks have always been used to guide the masses and manipulate truths to serve a purpose.

Powerlessness and our relationship to it has been passed down both individually and collectively, and how we live our lives mirrors our relationship to that state of being.

When we are in that space, desperation becomes our ally as it transmutes any sense of isolation, loneliness, and devastation.

We rush toward any panacea that will alleviate our fears. Our perceptions of right and wrong become distorted and part of a personal story of survival subjective to those fears.

Humanity is on a merry-go-round right now.

What one sees as the light, another perceives as the darkness and vice versa.

I want to step off that merry-go-round for a moment.

I want to silence my mind, be in my powerlessness, and allow it to tell its own story without my interference.

Would anybody like to join me?

◆ ◆ ◆

It is better to walk barefoot than with the wrong pair of shoes.

◆ ◆ ◆

I remember the day shame knelt in front of me and told me she was ready to move on. I asked her why, and she said I didn't need her anymore. She wanted me to forgive myself. Yes, it was that simple. All I needed to do was give myself permission.

The greatest revenge against any adversary is to become of service to humanity.

♦ ♦ ♦

The imprints you make on the earth will forever impact your ancestors before you and those to follow. If you think that the heavens did not see this coming; think again. If we look at this great shift as an opportunity to suffer, then it will be. If we look at this great shift as an opportunity to serve, then our suffering will be transformed.

♦ ♦ ♦

The truth shall set you free once you allow your attachments and ego to find another place to call home.

♦ ♦ ♦

My emotions are my responsibility.

Your reactions to them are yours.

What happens in the space between us takes enormous courage so that we may be honest with ourselves about our inner challenges, how we relate to them, and how our internal dialogue influences our external one.

May we all find the strength to hold that space for a moment longer, without judgment, and with the knowing that what we do in those moments of contemplation will have profound effects on every relationship we have.

♦ ♦ ♦

One who has a fear of intimacy has a greater fear of knowing him- or herself than knowing another.

◆ ◆ ◆

The unknown *is* the path.

◆ ◆ ◆

God awaits us in the midst of the forest—lush and verdant, tender with life's most reverent of creations. We cannot hear the cries of the greatest Mother of all. The Divine Feminine that settles beneath our flesh and bones, the womb Goddess, the carrier of all humankind. The epitome of grace made manifest by the heavens. These lands were birthed for the innocent, not for the iniquities hidden by the false desires we perpetuate in our minds. These lands were birthed for the holy, not for the entitled who endeavor to diminish any sanctity through greed, fear, anger, or any emotion that tears this womb apart. These lands await patiently. The kingdoms that dwell within this Great Mother have created sanctuaries for us to pray in, yet our lack of humility has made us uninvited guests at times. The trees whisper, but we cannot hear their stories. The flowers sing, but we cannot hear their music. The waters flow, but we refuse to value their importance. The animals protect and serve all kingdoms, yet we offer them no dignity. The only dignity some of us understand is that of our own self-righteousness. The earth was not created to serve humankind. It is we humans who were made to serve this Great Mother. How can we tread softly on her if we cannot even tread softly on the ground between one human being and the next? Our footprints will carry the tears of humanity as well as these lands. We will succumb to humility, and we can do it gently or be moved by the forces of Creation. We are feeling the movement that comes with rebirth. We are noticing the changes within all the kingdoms of this Great Mother. We are noticing the changes within humanity. The Divine Feminine is ready to birth anew. Are you?

◆ ◆ ◆

Not every mountain is meant to be climbed.

Some are there to be simply observed with the understanding that limitations are inherent tools for personal growth.

◆ ◆ ◆

Practice forgiveness until you no longer seek it outside of yourself.

◆ ◆ ◆

One of the greatest challenges you will ever face is the struggle against your own unworthiness.

◆ ◆ ◆

Shame begins in the spiritual womb when we first separate from the Divine. Then it becomes instinctual, psychological, emotional, and behavioral. Much time is wasted on unworthiness. How much suffering will you endure until you realize you are loved?

◆ ◆ ◆

From the moment we began to use language, emotions took on a whole different meaning and sensation. One of those emotions that has withstood the test of time is shame. Individual, societal, cultural, and collective, shame is both an inner and outer experience that lessens us in both our human and spiritual selves. It is a culmination of unworthiness, rejection, dehumanization, abandonment of one's true nature . . . the list can go on. It has been used since the dawn of time to manipulate human consciousness so that individuals and societies can continue to separate themselves from each other. It has been used to desensitize and devalue our Divinity as children of God. Shame compels human beings to seek a power outside of themselves, one that provides a false sense of empowerment and entitlement. This cycle of illusion continues throughout families and cultures, yet people flock to this emotion as though it were a shield of protection.

It is such a wound in our world, and yet the power it wields is enough to destroy the very foundations we have created as human beings to exist.

I don't ask that we destroy this emotion. I don't ask that we negate its power. I simply ask that we stop utilizing it as a source of empowerment. I ask that we seek to understand shame for the medicine it can offer us. I ask that we not allow shame to navigate our thoughts, our authenticity, the ways we love and live our lives.

There are other ways to feel empowered, achieve empowerment and empower others. There are other ways to feel love and give love. Shame can live in the silence of humanity; a healing medicine when appropriate, but not a code of honor we live by each day.

◆ ◆ ◆

Keep defining us by your projections, and we will only become more radiant. The healers, the artists, the witches, the soothsayers, the earthkeepers, the creators of imaginary worlds, who for centuries were held accountable for humankind's darkness. Our souls bound by light to discern the realms of existence and experience through visionary works, those seen and unseen. We are not here to harm but to share in the magic of the Divine and weave into this laden world stories of hope. Stories that will comfort the wounded, carry the oppressed, honor the wronged, praise the good, forgive the broken. We will never disappear. Our acts of kindness will echo through the hearts of many and engage distant lands, both above and below the heavens, until the day comes when you finally accept your place. You are also a creator of an imaginary world. We bask in the same realms. You are the healer, the artist, the witch, the soothsayer, and the earthkeeper. You cannot define your human or spiritual experience without acknowledging that we have woven our experiences to mirror each other. I am in you, and you are in me. Our stories dwell in the house of the gods as equals.

◆ ◆ ◆

May our souls seek the unknown
In the stillness where God resides,
Where conflict ceases to perpetuate itself
amidst humans not understanding His grace.
May the unknown nurture our humility
So that forgiveness becomes our truth.

3

COURAGE AND GRACE

C ourage is not the absence of fear, but the respect of it.

◆ ◆ ◆

Remember gently all that you have lost to despair.

Your memories contain a holiness, yet are bound by projections of individual and collective emotions that run wild with fear until they no longer recognize that sanctity of the Divine.

Scattered like ashes, your previous lives and those who came before you dwell in your memories and await a reunion like no other.

What is lost to despair waits patiently for you to gather yourself.

But the old ways of gathering are disappearing into the unknown, where reason defies your internal universe and what is required of you is a courage beyond your truth.

This courage will challenge any remnants of self you hold on fiercely to, waiting for the ashes to settle until you rise, purged from those ashes.

Not as individual but as a collective form, embodying the Divine and all its manifestations of Creation—one memory, one hope for all humanity and the heavens alike.

◆ ◆ ◆

I remember the day I no longer became frightened of my grief.

It was standing there like an old friend, a whisper away beyond the veil, holding hands with every one of my ancestors

Reminding me that it too made this journey of a thousand lifetimes to be my friend,

Reminding me not of every pain endured in my lineage, but of every sacrifice made to become whole,

To feel love, and to give love. To live.

I hope you never leave me, old friend.

◆ ◆ ◆

Some will know truth,
Some will speak truth,
Some will hide truth,
And some will simply live it.

◆ ◆ ◆

Embodied

To this earth realm that you endeavor to escape from.

To your wounded bodies that yearn for astral travel far and beyond your discernible senses.

So that any aspect of self that remains is entranced by elementals that alleviate your suffering.

Come back, dear children.

To this place of density that needs you so right now.

To this place of rooted beings within Creation deemed as sacred by the gods as the heavens.

To this place of madness that can only be remedied by the beauty you perceive amidst its complexities.

Yes, you will be wounded time and time again.

You will also be glorified and sanctified, connected to every living creature the stars shine their light upon.

Come back, dear children.

To this place of density, this place you and your ancestors call home.

For everything that is of earth is of you.

♦ ♦ ♦

This rain needs no introduction as it thrashes outside my window.

Its presence is as fierce as any archangel in heaven, yielding a sword to fight darkness in its midst.

Its energies compel me to hold still within myself, listening softly to its wisdom not spoken in words, but in its rapture.

As an augur it portends what is about to come.

I yield to its might, for it knows the secret mysteries of the universe within every drop of water,

Shedding the weight of humanity as it bears down upon us.

One secret at a time.

One portal at a time.

I surrender and press my womb against you as you evoke both God and Goddess in me, yearning to be healed by your magical waters.

I surrender.

♦ ♦ ♦

When you become as naked and vulnerable as the earth, you will know such humility and compassion that your tears will become rivers nourishing all of humanity's needs.

♦ ♦ ♦

Sometimes I prefer the company of spirits and angels over humans who choose not to love.

◆ ◆ ◆

The thunder outside my window is filled with such Presence.
A Presence gone wild in the throws of stillness
As transient souls wield their swords
And tend to the awakening of all humanity.
A thunder so powerful, I will weep until it hears my tears
And carries my soul across thresholds
Into a new Garden of Eden
Where I will dance with the Gods until every story in Creation is heard.
Take me, thunder, into your abode.
I want to be wild with you.
I want to be still with you.
I want to be one with you.

◆ ◆ ◆

As long as the wind is by my side, I don't need to move mountains. I can fly over them. Carried by her nurturance, softened by her faith, the wind becomes my mother, my sister, my child, my friend, believing in me those times I may not believe in myself. She is my ally in the natural world, whose light soothes the rawness of my being. Ever so gently, I reach for you, dear wind, when the air is unsettled. Knowing I will find you waiting for me, as we tread humbly across the stillness of the heavens in search of our next adventure.

◆ ◆ ◆

Become the void so you fear it less when you stumble upon it.

◆ ◆ ◆

We are all in the midst of an internal revolution to embrace a story of love that was woven for us long before we were ever born.

◆ ◆ ◆

Enter into yourself with the sun shining upon your face and holy ground beneath your feet.

◆ ◆ ◆

Inhabit yourself first before taking up residence in other people's lives.

◆ ◆ ◆

The magnitude of that storm yesterday,
Bending all to its will,
Purification at its height of magnificence.
Lost souls yearning to be entrenched in its grasp
As it cleansed the ethers of impurities no longer needed by our present construct.
We will be molded by nature.
An instrument of grace we have yet to appreciate,
Under the tutelage of the gods,
Showing mercy in ways we do not understand.

◆ ◆ ◆

And God said, "Let there be light."
    I turned askance and told Her not yet.
    I wanted to sit with my darkness for a while and let it show me what I needed to learn about myself.
    God paused for a moment and then smiled.
    She granted me a kindness I would not understand until the time was right.

♦ ♦ ♦

I can't tell you you will always feel safe.

I can't tell you you will never feel alone.

I can't tell you life will be easy.

I can't tell you you will never suffer.

I can't tell you you will always feel like you belong.

I can't tell you you will never feel like you are at the edge of that precipice, teetering on the brink of exhaustion.

What I can tell you is this—you are loved and held in a grace so palpable beyond any realm you could ever perceive that any thoughts of separation you feel during this earthly existence will be but a distant memory once you remember you are of the light.

♦ ♦ ♦

When you have outgrown your story in your healing process, there will be people in your life who want to hold you back; people who are afraid of change, afraid of the person you will become outside of that story. They are afraid that the new story you have created might no longer have space for them inside of it. They have the choice to welcome your new beginning into their lives as a blessing and make those changes that will invite them into your new narrative. Choice is powerful.

♦ ♦ ♦

Once shame availed itself to me, I introduced it to one of my closest friends—forgiveness. From that moment on, one ceased to exist without the other.

♦ ♦ ♦

The greatest home you will ever live in is the one inside your own heart.

♦ ♦ ♦

I tried to walk away from my fear until one day it reached for my hand and told me how much it wanted to learn from my light.

◆ ◆ ◆

I remember the day God told me I was beautiful. All those parts of myself I disliked just melted away in Her arms.

◆ ◆ ◆

Human decency embodied awakens us to the intricacies of each person's struggles, allowing us to understand how another person could live their life differently from what we might expect of them.

It gives ground to our own insecurities, igniting a deeper understanding of the collective within, of the power struggle every human being has with other human beings, of that inner struggle to be validated, acknowledged, received on such a level where the "us versus them" paradigm ceases to exist. Where someone's light is not judged to be better than another.

Where everyone's darkness is offered a mercy and the opportunity to rise above.

I sometimes witness people being afraid of embodying this, as though in giving too much they will be faced with an ominous emptiness.

I just know this: when embodied, the need to compare your own struggles to someone else's will dissipate.

Your hand and heart extended to your neighbor will be the same hand and heart that give you breath and feed your life.

◆ ◆ ◆

Sometimes you just need to bask in the wilderness of your own heart to set yourself free.

◆ ◆ ◆

I remember the day I realized just how powerful love could be.

I turned to the heavens and whispered in God's ears, "Thank you."

I reached for the soft earth beneath my feet, and the same words flowed from my breath:

"Thank you."

Then I took my hands and caressed this tired body, which has carried my spirit, and smiled.

The words flowed effortlessly, accompanied by tears rolling down my cheeks as I knelt to that same soft earth, touching her, touching me. I gazed at my body and held her gently and repeated over and over again, "Thank you."

◆ ◆ ◆

When grief inhabits your body, it sojourns in every living cell until one of your ancestors reaches out to it and wipes the tears off its visage.

◆ ◆ ◆

There's that moment we realize our feelings of unworthiness have influenced every relationship we've ever had in this lifetime, including the one we have with ourselves. There's that moment we realize we could have discerned things differently if we were more gentle with our being. Then there comes *that* moment; the one in which we come to the greater understanding that it's all about choice. The choice to love or the choice to allow our unworthiness to continue to devalue our human and spiritual potential, individually and collectively, until we no longer recognize ourselves as children of grace. I choose to love.

◆ ◆ ◆

A heart uncompromised understands gratitude without words and appreciates life's sacredness in its entirety.

♦ ♦ ♦

Remind me of my own holiness in times when I am lost without You.

♦ ♦ ♦

The possibility of having your inner chaos surrender to your inner silence is greater than you could ever imagine.

♦ ♦ ♦

If someone is continually disappointed in you, their perceptions of who you are in this world do not meet their expectations. How unfortunate for them that they struggle so.

♦ ♦ ♦

Sometimes you need to be the storm that challenges still waters whose patterns are resistant to change.

♦ ♦ ♦

Chaos can understand kindness more than it can resentment. Choose your battles wisely.

♦ ♦ ♦

Enchained and shackled by fear
Only to be freed by grace.
I promise.

♦ ♦ ♦

The Holy Land is not a place one travels to. It is the place one arrives at when standing in stillness.

♦ ♦ ♦

You don't chase dreams. You live them. You chase illusion.

♦ ♦ ♦

When the mountain seemed too difficult to climb, I told God I needed a new path to walk on. He told me all I needed was to change my shoes.

◆ ◆ ◆

Some might say you are not enough.
Others will say you are just too much.
How lonely an experience for those who spend time measuring the worth of others through the guise of their own self-contempt.

◆ ◆ ◆

That moment you realize you are "enough," every relationship you have in this world will change, including the one with yourself.

◆ ◆ ◆

You are greater than any weakness you deem yourself to have because of your ability to relate to it from a nonreactive, non-judgmental, and neutral heart.

◆ ◆ ◆

What I learned through chaos gave me the courage to be present within the silence.

◆ ◆ ◆

I look for courage among the meek, as they are humbly unaware of their own strength at times. They shall rise in the kingdom of heaven, so let us show kindness toward them on earth.

◆ ◆ ◆

She stood there motionless, not sure which path to follow. She stood there anxiously, waiting to feel the presence of the Divine embrace her. When all the while, she hadn't even realized that God actually never let go of her hand.

Then she heard a voice whisper in her ear, "Follow Me. No matter which road we take I will make sure you end up where you are supposed to be. It may not be easy, but if you have faith in Me, I will give you the greatest strength and courage you have ever known." So she began to move slowly. And with that her trust grew in baby steps, as did her sense of self. Then her compassion followed and, with that, a love of humanity that she never would have imagined.

◆ ◆ ◆

The power in believing you are enough will impact your life in ways you could never imagine.

◆ ◆ ◆

When most people think of the word "inadequate," what comes to mind is not being good enough. It indeed has its roots in self-worth, self-identity, shame, and loss.

Loss alters one's mind and heart when identity is left to be unearthed by psychological, emotional, and societal paradigms; by aspects of the psyche that are ingrained from the time we are in the womb through the norms of social and behavioral development. The aura of innocence becomes skewed as we mature from babies to children and, individually and collectively, take on the wounds of those around us and those who came before us. The holiness many of us know on such a deep level becomes enmeshed in our thoughts of who we should be, who we aren't, and what we might never become. That holiness never fades; it is simply forgotten as we become programmed toward establishing an identity that suits external influences in our lives. Those influences become internalized, setting up a pattern in which thoughts of "not being good enough" or "not being enough" get challenged on a daily basis. I am okay with those thoughts if they take you further inside yourself to become reacquainted with your holiness. Most of the time those thoughts continue to separate us from ourselves and the world around us. Those thoughts then set the precedent for much of the hatred we experience within and between race, sexual orientation, religion, and all relationships, including the one we have with ourselves. Our feelings of inadequacy can feel overwhelming and propel us into a state of powerlessness. We feel like we have no control over who or what we are or who or what others perceive us to be. It is an addictive emotional spiral that takes us down the rabbit hole searching for something that has actually never left us. Beyond the shame, beyond the loss, beyond the powerlessness, there is an identity that has yet to be discovered within ourselves. An identity that, when embraced, raises inadequacy to a state of enlightenment that desires to be respected. Not for the hurt it can do, but for the self-realization it offers us through that place of holiness. That gentle place, where identity meets the Divine. That place where we are held as much as we do the holding for ourselves and each other. Identity takes on a whole new meaning when we walk hand in hand with our holiness, and inadequacy becomes part of that holiness.

◆ ◆ ◆

Sometimes those who keep reminding you to let go are the ones who hold on the most.

◆ ◆ ◆

The healing might be just as invisible as the wound. You may not know it until one day you simply realize you are not suffering in those same ways you are used to.

◆ ◆ ◆

Our vulnerabilities do not lead us astray. Our shame of them does.

♦ ♦ ♦

Never stop being amazed at how much you can endure.

♦ ♦ ♦

There will come a time when your inner silence no longer frightens you.

♦ ♦ ♦

May we all learn that gentleness becomes a warrior too.

♦ ♦ ♦

Don't allow your perception of who you are to alter your experience of becoming.

♦ ♦ ♦

Meet failure with an intimate sense of worthiness and you will have succeeded in a far greater capacity than you ever imagined.

♦ ♦ ♦

Tread prayerfully amidst the souls of others. You just might be walking amongst angels.

♦ ♦ ♦

Just because you don't understand someone else's life doesn't mean his or her story is not worth being heard.

♦ ♦ ♦

The moment we think our light is greater than another's is the moment our darkness reveals itself.

♦ ♦ ♦

The capacity for hatred is such a learned behavior amidst the collective. We as individuals have to approach the healing of such with a communal effort, no longer as a solitary work of inner reflection. The transgenerational trauma surrounding such hatred has been passed down mentally, physically, and spiritually. As times have changed, so has our relationship to this collective hatred. Internalized experiences, cultural norms, and inherited psychological patterns of dealing with traumatic events all shape the way we learn to hate, the way we carry it, the ways in which we express it, and the ways in which we are given the opportunities to heal from it. We are at a crossroads in history in every realm of existence and experience. Healing collectively is no longer a choice; it is a necessity. The individual wound is but a moment in linear time. The collective wound in nonlinear time is what we are in the midst of experiencing now. The only way to move forward is together.

◆ ◆ ◆

May your inner wild shine again.

◆ ◆ ◆

You are not broken.

You were made in Her image and likeness to withstand the darkness.

You were made to endure His rapture within your soul for all eternity.

You were made to endure the woundings of all humanity, if only to heal each other across time.

You were made to experience such intensity of raw emotion, stripping every facet of your being until you are left humbled to your knees, receiving such intimate grace that it raises you back up on angel's wings.

You are not broken.

You are a child of God, the universe, the earth that carries you.

You are children of one another. You cannot be broken as long as you remember you are one.

❖ ❖ ❖

Walk gently out of the silence
From that sacred tabernacle you call home
Into the chaos of illusion, where thoughts and emotions run rampant with abandon.
Where any sense of self becomes a mystery
Unrecognized by that same silence that beckons your return.
That same silence you chose to leave to enter into illusion.
Did you find what you were looking for?

❖ ❖ ❖

Sometimes limitations are an expression of a boundary the universe needs to set for a far greater purpose than we realize. In this world, our limitations can feel constricting, frightening, and endless. In other realms, those same limitations might heal, console, or remedy a miasm that has been waiting for its next evolutionary shift to happen. The more respectful we are of a limitation imposed upon us by the universe, the more fluid the shift will be in both worlds. Trust the process.

❖ ❖ ❖

Sometimes we need to look at limitations as the boundary we didn't know we needed until the lesson was learned.

❖ ❖ ❖

Into the wild I go, where my fears are tamed by the Divine only to surrender to all that is deemed Holy.

✦ ✦ ✦

There are times God takes you gently by the hand. It might feel like a soft breeze whispering through your hair, letting you know over and over again just how much you are loved. Be open to Her touch, and you will never know loneliness again.

✦ ✦ ✦

Grief has a way of grounding you further into yourself, in spaces you never knew existed inside your being. It has a way of settling into your bones and challenging your experience of living, loving, and letting go. Your relationship with grief will be one of the most influential relationships you will ever have in this lifetime. Carry it well.

Make every rite of passage embolden you to honor every moment.

✦ ✦ ✦

Raw and untamed, we enter into this world, this wilderness, birthed from a womb that has carried the stories of many generations. Unfiltered psyche, present in parallel realities as we are ensconced by a knowing of the life to come. We are still in the water, waiting to be born, to be nurtured as much by humanity as we are the Divine, not having any preconceived notions of what that might look like. All we pray for is to be welcomed by this vast wilderness we are entering into, this human conglomeration of emotions, thoughts, experiences, prayers. This wilderness is perplexing. Masculine and feminine energies abound, compelling us to mold into a form governed by what humans think they should be. This wilderness has an evolution all its own. One that, many times, we are not ready to embrace. One that, many times, we are not willing to accept. Our vulnerabilities are channeled through the forms that are presented us. What do we know, coming from innocence? We are vulnerable in our fears. We are vulnerable in our anger. We are vulnerable in our capacity to love. We are vulnerable in our capacity to hate. Our innocence is frightened away by our emotional projections, yet how can we not project? The iniquities of this world challenge us to the bone. We separate ourselves in this wilderness; any identity we need to feel safe, innocent, whole. The wilderness is meant to inspire us to feel, to live, to lose our sense of selves so that we may become greater than we ever thought we could be. This wilderness compels us to feel lost, to grieve so deeply that our bones ache with each step we take. And with every step, we cradle ourselves unto the earth for solace, for healing. This wilderness compels us to feel our rage, one that many of us do not know how to channel correctly. One that we utilize to destroy one another and hurt the very earth that carries us. Naked, in our aloneness, this wilderness does not want us to suffer. We feel stalked by a darkness we cannot comprehend. Yet if we turn around to see exactly what might be stalking us, we'll be staring at a mirror of ourselves.

The sacredness of this wilderness can balance that darkness without any interference from humanity, from our projections onto one another. Naked and alive, wild and free, the resilience and innocence we were born with can indeed be remembered. They can be remembered as easily as the many tears we have shed for our wounds. We possess the courage, the innate fire of the Divine, to explore our emptiness in this vast paradigm. We possess the strength to go beyond the identity we were born with or have created for ourselves. We possess the worthiness as children of this God-blessed natural world to honor our grief, our rage, and any other emotion that limits us, that armors us, from loving one another unconditionally. Emerging from the water, unto this rare earth, with its stories and paths of generations before us. Their emotions, their thoughts, still present when we lay our armor to the ground. Their spirits, still weaving an intricate web to amend past grievances and future ones to come. That untamed fire, that innocence, the loss of self, all culminating in an intense desire to be free from all preconceived notions of who we think we are, and how we live our lives. Wild, free, innocent, beautiful children of God. Bless you. Return to innocence and be free.

◆ ◆ ◆

God met me in the wild of the spirit world where I was born.

She tamed me in the womb of my mother.

She birthed me into a world where the wild of the spirit world now seemed so sacred and silent.

If only I knew then what I know now.

Back to the silent wilderness one day I will go.

Where spirits are tamed by a love so magnificent they spend their entire earthly existence searching for it.

Back to the sacred silence. Where all things wild are free.

◆ ◆ ◆

There is that one pivotal moment before you surrender when you look back at the darkness and wonder if you should stay because it is so familiar. Some might tremble with uncertainty; others might exhale in anticipation of freedom. We all come to that place every day in our lives. These choices are not always easy, but rest assured we are always held in those moments.

◆ ◆ ◆

As the Mystery unfolds, may we gently unfold with it so we no longer see ourselves as separate from the Divine.

◆ ◆ ◆

The slower you walk in your shadow, the more gracious you will be of your light when you come upon it.

♦ ♦ ♦

The moment you believe the world owes you something is the moment you've lost faith in the larger purpose behind your battles.

♦ ♦ ♦

I am not afraid of the fire as long as the Divine is lighting the match.

♦ ♦ ♦

There is a powerful threshold when one is standing within the crossroads of the light. We can become so assured that we are resting in the presence of the Divine or the Creator, yet the ego and our attachments forget we are still embodied in human form. Until we have crossed that threshold, we are still responsible for our relationship to self, others, the world, and the heavens.

Even in the spirit world, those who have traveled through various dimensions still seek solace and peace within their spirit bodies. Evolution does not stop when we cross into other worlds. In fact, it becomes even more important. Whether you stand within the Holy Trinity, honor the Four Directions, or are an integral part of any other spiritual tradition that has afforded every human being the right to find peace within his or her humanity, the integration of ancestral and world lineages rests solely on the free will we all have to live our lives with respect for those spiritual laws that unite us in all worlds.

♦ ♦ ♦

Unconditional love sometimes requires boundaries we never even knew we had until we come to that moment when all that we think we know about ourselves disappears into oblivion. Many of us enter into relationship seeking to define ourselves and a perceived reality or realities we have created since we were birthed into this world. Seeking to define humanity and the Divine within relationship takes courage, sacrifice, patience, and surrender. Many have a thought that unconditional love translates into having no boundaries. In my limited experience, the presence of self requires a purification one can only undergo walking through Creation in aloneness. It is within this space that our projections of who we perceive we are and how we perceive our relationships will be quieted. Boundaries are formed many times by reactions and responses to life's experiences. Those boundaries may indeed be appropriate in that moment, but those reactions and responses become programmed into cellular memory if they have not already arisen from those spaces. For a boundary to grow and emerge without interference from thoughts and emotions, that quiet space, that pause, that pivotal moment for renewed awakening of self-creation has to be ignited. And from my experience, that alone time where you come into relationship with yourself is so extremely important. That alone time where you become friends with your inner knowing, with your ego, with your heart, your mind and your spirit. That alone time where you befriend your sense of powerlessness and empowerment. That alone time where you define yourself outside of the constructs you have created, eventually leading to a place where the need to define yourself is not as important as it used to be. And this is because there is a flow of energy between you and God in embracing a profound respect for this life you were given.

In this space, unconditional love is received as a blessing, and we are each given the opportunity to understand how to share this gift with one another. We are each given the opportunity to understand how to place appropriate boundaries when needed, not out of reaction or any other emotion that distracts us from our true nature, but out of Divine Providence. We shift our understanding of relationships from codependency to interdependency on both the human and spiritual levels. We were taught to continue the illusion of codependency. We were taught to continue the illusion of unworthiness. We were taught to continue the illusion of self-sacrifice to the extent that we no longer remember the wholeness and sanctity in which sacrifice has an *entirely* different meaning. We were born to create interdependent relationships here on earth, as are the relationships created in the heavens. I have a thought that our boundary systems are so wounded from lifetimes of confusion. There is so much separation from the boundaries of the world we live in today. May we be given the strength to discern sacrifice from both a human and a spiritual perspective and create a boundary that will enrich the lives of everyone fostering unconditional love as only God would have it.

◆ ◆ ◆

I prefer to be in the company of the unknown rather than in the company of ignorance.

◆ ◆ ◆

Reach into oblivion and there you will find me.

Not as you would have me, but as I deem best for your greatest good, your greatest love, and your greatest worth.

◆ ◆ ◆

May unprecedented fear lead to unprecedented awakening.

◆ ◆ ◆

Move freely within your own sacredness. That which is contained is held together by a Providence so Divine.

♦ ♦ ♦

The darkness harkens for the light—

Wading through rivers of confusion for centuries, yearning to be touched by a grace whose acquaintance it has never met before.

Slowly, it emerges out of chaos, only to realize the light had been holding its hand the entire time.

The light calls herself grace.

♦ ♦ ♦

The fall from grace is momentary. The rise to holiness is eternal.

♦ ♦ ♦

Find your container, have a stronger boundary, and let movement of grace flow through you, and may the darkness be your shelter as well but contained within the tabernacle of grace so it doesn't feel as heavy as you perceive it to be. You can do this. You have survived through much. Amazing when we let go of the story and just let the energy serve and go where it needs to go. The more story you let go of, the more quiet will come.

♦ ♦ ♦

When the wind howls like this I can hear almost every name of my ancestors. Their voices call to me with comfort and reassurance of the past, wisdom for the present, and discernment for the future. Their names have become powerful for my lineage, just as the names for your lineage strengthen you in times of weakness. Call them by their energies if names are not known. Feel their presence embrace the womb we are all being birthed from. The wind howling, the womb contracting, rebirth, newness, the unknown, eternity. I am going to listen to the wind again now, to hear more names I have never heard before, to feel more energies unbeknownst to me. Move me, wind. Carry me from this womb into the unexpected journey that awaits me.

♦ ♦ ♦

The light doesn't diminish the darkness. It simply helps it to understand its true nature.

♦ ♦ ♦

Heart is where your home is. If you find your home empty, open your heart.

♦ ♦ ♦

If we deem the nexus between the individual and the collective as rooted in separation, then we will continue to perpetuate a cycle of illusion.

We choose ignorance over insight because we believe it mitigates suffering. We choose inadequacy over authenticity to keep us from looking within. What is familiar has become safe for many of us, even if it means betraying all that we know to be good and holy. Fear has become a reactive response to life's experience. The fear in and of itself is not a negative thing. How we carry the fear and allow it to demean our inner lives, how we allow it to demean our connection with others and with the Divine keeps us from experiencing that holiness. We are all at a crossroads, heaven and earth, in choosing to allow grace to permeate our lives the way that it is intended, not in the ways in which we feel safe in receiving it. Abandoning those thoughts that keep the illusion alive is something we can all do together. Receiving grace is perhaps one of the most sacred experiences of our humanity. Shall we begin?

♦ ♦ ♦

Mastering the illusion requires realization that in some way we have created it.

♦ ♦ ♦

Walk with me into nowhere, where emptiness has its rightful place amidst the heavens.

Where tears are comforted amidst understanding.

Where Presence is felt when you don't know where you belong.

Where fear is held in sanctity of what lessons it can offer you.

Walk with me into nowhere, where my soul reaches into yours and no boundary exists except the ones that our minds create.

Where my soul touches upon yours, the lightness of our own beings, so much so that any separation would be unbearable.

Walk with me into nowhere, where you and I exist as one, not tearing each other apart to survive a reality that is only experienced by our projections.

Where you and I exist as one, emotions running fluidly through sparks of matter that ground our souls into dense, earthly bodies.

Held by a container we call love, leaving little room for thoughts, which continue to separate.

Walk with me into nowhere.

I will find you.

You will find me.

How could we not?

After all, we are one, and nowhere is the tabernacle of the gods.

♦ ♦ ♦

Becoming who you were meant to be takes much more effort than being who you thought you were.

♦ ♦ ♦

I don't want to be sheltered from the storm. I want to be shelter *for* that storm. May its power find refuge amidst my own strength. May its chaos find balance within my courage. May its intensity find stillness within my light.

♦ ♦ ♦

May innocence be your refuge in times of uncertainty.

♦ ♦ ♦

Some people call them dreams.
    Others call them nightmares.
    Some see good where there is evil.
    Others see evil where there is good.
    Some call it fate or destiny.
    Others call it choice.
    The simplest shift in perception yields a power so great it can alter any reality we imagine ourselves in.
    Illusion and reality lose their meaning in stillness, where perceptions surrender to an unknown force greater than anything we are capable of discerning.

♦ ♦ ♦

Between good and evil lies this place so empowering, it is called stillness.

♦ ♦ ♦

Tend to your life delicately in this time of contemplation. Isolation can yield such a hunger for power during those times we feel conquered. What was lost does not necessarily have to be found again. You did not lose your way. You lost yourself. The way never left you. When you finally see that, you will contemplate life differently, and what has held you back will now stand at your side in humility as you move forward.

◆ ◆ ◆

Your bitterness is not the issue. How it influences your path is. Forgive.

◆ ◆ ◆

A story never told may not have the chance to be rewritten. Now is your time.

◆ ◆ ◆

When everyone is in the midst of their own story, they may not be able to see your story in the way you hope it is seen.

◆ ◆ ◆

"Dance with me," God said to fear.
"I'm afraid," fear replied.
"Of what?"
"That I may see your light."

◆ ◆ ◆

The extraordinary lives within each of us.

Cultivate the extraordinary from the ordinary, as insignificance has no place within your mind.

◆ ◆ ◆

A life that we take for granted is not a life at all. It is a prison in which we are held by beliefs that further the illusion that the darkness and that which fuels it is the key to humanity's survival. One cannot survive on darkness alone, especially a darkness that does not yield to the light in which all truths carry equal weight for all humanity.

♦ ♦ ♦

The Divine has taken such extraordinary measures to make us human. Oh, how we squander the opportunity with much folly!

♦ ♦ ♦

May today's prayer be tomorrow's grace.

♦ ♦ ♦

When you leave little room for grace to enter your life, you will come to know sorrow more times than you could imagine.

♦ ♦ ♦

In stillness you will be reborn.

♦ ♦ ♦

In these times of uncertainty, be someone's reason for finding faith in a Higher Power.

♦ ♦ ♦

When your gentle spirit ignites someone's anger, remain in stillness so they could be reminded of the inner peace they are longing for.

♦ ♦ ♦

The ancient womb is awakening.

Impatience is rising, as is frustration. The universal womb is contracting, ready to give birth to all of us, to this new paradigm that was seen and known by the ancient ones. This new womb is awakening with fervor and passion, strength and a determination to gather collectively to heal in ways we have not understood before. The ancients understood. It is we who have been sleeping, cradling ourselves in this materialistic and linear construct mentally, psychologically, emotionally, and spiritually. Many have focused on doing the inner work of the soul yet somewhere in the midst, the notion of simplicity of the Divine, of Holy Providence, of the spiritual laws of the Universe have been lost to oblivion. We are all wanting to vibrate to a higher frequency so badly that the simplicity of love and our relationship to it becomes so ensconced that we may fail to recognize the Divine in everything within and around us. Our unyielding search for this profound Holiness takes us away from being present.

The path is right here, right now. The Divine is right here, right now. You are right here, right now. Whether we are conscious or not, the Divine still works through us in both seen and unseen ways. Engaging the search for the path out of desire to achieve enlightenment carries many attachments. The ripples are being felt as our attachments are being challenged, because what we thought we envisioned for this new year may not manifest in the ways we had intended. Your womb is held by the universal womb. The ripples being felt are at such an intensity that many are left questioning if they are headed in the right direction. The anxieties being felt are because we are all ready to be birthed anew. If we hold on to the old understandings of our purpose in this world, we will struggle. If we allow for ourselves to move into Presence, our purpose will be revealed. And if the purpose is familiar to you, the way you carry it into the world will be different. This ancient womb carries many mysteries. Some will be revealed individually as we embark on our journeys, some will be revealed collectively, and some mysteries will remain forever in the house of the gods serving a purpose we humans might never comprehend.

◆ ◆ ◆

In your grace I become healed.
In your grace I become holy.
In your grace I become strong.
In your grace I become fearless.
In your grace I become kind.
In your grace I become peaceful.
In your grace I become patient.
In your grace I become truthful.
In your grace I become powerful.
In your grace I become humbled.
In your grace I become Divine.

4

THE PAUSE

There will always be a place for you, my love
Amidst a vibrant and lush earth
Whose windswept landscape, made luminescent by the
elements of the gods,
Takes you by the hand and holds you by the heart,
Whose pulsating breath moves through you softly,
Entering into your holiness
One heartbeat at a time,
Waiting for you to receive its splendor.
With all your trepidation,
You exhale slowly, opening to its benevolence.
This wondrous earth.
A home unlike any you have witnessed before,
Except that of your own soul.
Treat it reverently.

There is a shared narrative among the stars that we humans
could only hope to understand. It is a love unparalleled between
galaxies where no star ever feels left alone.

◆ ◆ ◆

May every unkind word that comes your way be transformed by your heart into a prayer of love.

◆ ◆ ◆

I remember the day I asked God to show me how to be kind. She gently pointed to my heart and told me to begin by trusting in it.

◆ ◆ ◆

We will be uprooted to a degree that knows no human understanding of boundaries.

The earth underneath our feet will fold into itself until it softens into its destiny without any manipulation from human desire.

The awakening will make raw those places inside of us that are already wounded.

What was once written in the stars, spoken across galaxies, is unfolding now.

Within every cell of our existence, amidst every ancestor in our lineage, transformation is occurring.

So much so that we will not recognize humanity as we once knew it.

Those who hold onto what was will continue to sleep.

But the gods are whispering into our souls.

"Sleep no more, dear children. We are awakening as one."

◆ ◆ ◆

Drench us in love, Goddess divine, so we can feel your tenderness upon every inch of our flesh, making all our deepest wounds holy.

◆ ◆ ◆

One can live an extraordinary life within the silence.

♦ ♦ ♦

Claim your holiness in such a profound way that you have no desire to ever look back at the person you believed yourself to be.

♦ ♦ ♦

To uncreate illusion, you must first be willing to recognize that you are living in one.

♦ ♦ ♦

I crave the wilderness as much as I crave the silence.

♦ ♦ ♦

There is a poignant beauty to shattered glass. Each piece reveals its wholeness and its ability to sustain itself as separate from the others. It retains its character as its edges become more refined and strengthened through this process of separation. Understanding that in order to work through illusion, the importance of that which is broken is a minute aspect of a greater impermanent reality, where all parts serve a Higher good. The shattering therefore serves as illusion as well.

♦ ♦ ♦

My emptiness is mine to own, not yours to heal. Respect what we find within the silence.

♦ ♦ ♦

Navigating against the emptiness will not leave you as peaceful as flowing with it does.

♦ ♦ ♦

"Becoming" embraces the pause in between the need.

♦ ♦ ♦

Sometimes it takes great courage to be gentle with yourself.

♦ ♦ ♦

Sometimes the fall is the rise up.

♦ ♦ ♦

Meet me in the unknown. I will give you all the answers you desire in that stillness that frightens you so.

♦ ♦ ♦

The warrior understands that stillness can be his greatest weapon.

♦ ♦ ♦

When in doubt, seek stillness over movement. You will find it takes much less effort and offers greater reward.

♦ ♦ ♦

Seek refuge in the silence that birthed you into this human existence.

♦ ♦ ♦

I didn't know I was asleep until the Divine whispered in my ear to awaken.

♦ ♦ ♦

Your interior world is humbled by infinite graces you aren't even aware of yet.

♦ ♦ ♦

The awakened one slept for a while, perhaps many incarnations, before he awoke from his illusion.

♦ ♦ ♦

The wombs of many prepare for the birth of one. Our lives are an intricate part of the collective. Forget that and you lose sight of your own birth between worlds.

◆ ◆ ◆

When your darkness meets your light, that is a perfect time to pause. A response born out of desperation has the power to alter any path you set yourself on. The path does not create a relationship to desperation. It is your mind that does.

◆ ◆ ◆

When people leave your life, it's not because they can't be in your personal space. It's because they can't be in their own space while they are with you.

◆ ◆ ◆

God said, "Let there be light."
Well then . . .
First appeared the clouds.
Then the rains fell.
It soon began to storm.
Everywhere was flooded.
Cries of desperation could be heard from every corner of the earth.
Where was the light?
The light was the cloud.
It was indeed the abundant rain.
It transformed itself into that magnificent storm
And was seen shining brightly through the floods.
Oh how we perceive such trials.
Oh how we lose faith.
In the eyes of the Divine, those signs are merely greetings from Heaven

Letting you know all hope is not lost.
The light of Spirit is everywhere around you.
May we all perceive such trials as graces from the unseen.

♦ ♦ ♦

Eventually, as we heal, we arrive at a place beyond the story. The words that tell our stories become less powerful and the need to identify with those words less important. We move beyond interpretations, attachments, and any other vices that prevent us from experiencing the energies behind our stories that offer us that nourishment for healing. That sacred ground where words won't have the same power over you as they once did before. That sacred ground where you give yourself permission to see, feel, embrace, and understand your story in the ways you choose to. You will come to own your story and live it in ways you never did before. We all will.

♦ ♦ ♦

In times of chaos, may innocence be a source of strength.

♦ ♦ ♦

Sweeten those memories that have pained you with forgiveness.

♦ ♦ ♦

I have enough faith in you to move mountains even when you think they are standing still.

♦ ♦ ♦

May your past be offered a kindness it has never known so that your future meets every opportunity with grace.

♦ ♦ ♦

Change your perceptions of who you are within the emptiness, and you will change your life.

✦ ✦ ✦

The shift happens when your awakening reaches into the substance of your bones; when your flesh realizes with great authenticity that your humanity is as much about the change as is your divine self. Our earth element belongs as much to the gods as it does to the lower worlds, those worlds beneath your feet that feed our bodies as much as they feed our minds and spirits. Those worlds beneath our feet that root us into a depth of self that is unspoken. The shift happens when we least expect it, truly never leaving us with wanting more, as we lay in presence within the tabernacle of our own holiness.

✦ ✦ ✦

If you want to see the world, travel the landscape of your own heart.

✦ ✦ ✦

Be patient with your impatience.

Desperation is rising to heights within the unknown of self, neighbor, and reality; the only way through this is to be gentle with time itself.

Time is not the enemy, nor are those imposing limitations and constraints on your inner and outer worlds.

Your enemy is the inability to move fluidly within those limitations, to carry your emotions with some sanctity of inner peace, to maintain a level of understanding that a Higher Power does preside within us and around us. We have the opportunity to become human beings again. Some might wonder if we as a world ever were. Self-consumption of power, greed, and hate have obscured the very reason we arrived in this realm, which is simply to love. Simply to love.

◆ ◆ ◆

When you can no longer breathe, you will remember the cries of the earth being scorched due to man's ignorance and greed. It takes but one moment to show some mercy for our natural world and those whose footprints imprint themselves upon it. One moment, one act of kindness. We are not entitled to live here. We are privileged.

◆ ◆ ◆

God beckoned, and I grew wings. She made them strong enough for me to find my way home when I needed Her stillness.

◆ ◆ ◆

May the enormity of this world's darkness be healed one light at a time.

◆ ◆ ◆

Arise from the womb gently, child.
The nourishing waters will baptize you.
In all that is seen humanly,
In all that is unseen Divinely.
From the waters to the earth,
You will leave many remarkable imprints.
Some so soft, God will notice.
Others so harsh, you will cry.
Running back to the flowing waters,
To the womb that held you.
But there is no going back.
A new womb awaits you, child.
The waters are nothing you know.
You do not know yourself yet.
The waters will soon rise up.

You will come to know them
As you come into knowing yourself.
This womb will be very different.
You will baptize the nourishing waters.
You will give this womb strength.
You will make the womb holy.
You will make the unseen seen.
No more running toward safe haven.
You will be that safe haven.
You will be that sacred womb.

◆ ◆ ◆

The storm will come and go. Passing through you with enough of an intensity to humble your ego; wearing you down to a space of anonymity that is indescribable. Allow the storm to change you. Perhaps it will not even recognize the light of your own being the next time that same storm comes around again.

◆ ◆ ◆

May our emptiness be as forthcoming as our determination, so that we endeavor to remain humbled by gratitude.

◆ ◆ ◆

What you deem as sacred is what will carry you home.

◆ ◆ ◆

I am not who you think I am.

I am more than the flesh and bones that carry my soul upon this wayward earth.

I am a vessel; an imprint of imagination, desire, holiness, and creation begun long ago with my lineage.

I am a confluence of generations; of thought and emotion polarized by both my humanity and Divinity.

I am a memory long ago born and not yet created. I am the matrix upon which good and evil flow in balance to teach me humility and gratitude.

I am not who you think I am.

Nor am I who I perceive myself to be.

I am an eternity held in a linear reality until the time my flesh and bones dissolve into nothingness.

I am the "other" I see before me every waking moment.

I am the creation I stumble upon that only embodies form so I can understand.

I am the silence within the chaos. I am the chaos before that silence.

I am the grace from which these words flow.

I am more than that. And so are you. . . .

Eventually, I will no longer have an interest in wondering who I am.

I will no longer have an interest in wondering who you are.

We will carry each other as one in the silence of our being, already knowing we are borne of the same love, the same magnificence, the same grace. The silence will show us.

◆ ◆ ◆

I weep for souls who do not understand the extraordinary power of forgiveness. Don't let bitterness call your heart a home.

◆ ◆ ◆

The chaos doesn't change you. Your relationship to it does.

◆ ◆ ◆

An unattended soul leaves more space for darkness to enter.

◆ ◆ ◆

The deepest form of self-respect comes from having faith in a Higher Power.

◆ ◆ ◆

The moment I thought I had no more fight left in me, God put His hand upon my shoulder. I turned around to find solace in Her comfort, and there on the ground were my sword and my shield, reminding me the courage to be a warrior was only a prayer away.

◆ ◆ ◆

Evolution requires our conscious participation, not our projections.

◆ ◆ ◆

Be moved to tears by your own acts of kindness. Don't wait to witness them from others.

◆ ◆ ◆

Become inspired by your own destiny to actually see it through, no matter what challenges lie ahead of you.

◆ ◆ ◆

Exclusion begets tyranny. It begins with the womb and ends with the womb. We are all nourished by the same life-giving waters, carried through different vessels as made manifest by the Creator. Exclusion begins in family systems when we forget about mutual reciprocity, equality, and respect. Let *inclusion* be a pathway to healing, so that every womb births peace on earth through evolutionary beings.

◆ ◆ ◆

The moment you have allowed yourself to become hypnotized by another person's power is the moment you have let go of your own.

♦ ♦ ♦

May your days be comforted by the sun and your nights be softened by the moon. May the winds carry your prayers to the heavens while the clouds comfort your fears. May you be held completely by this gentle earth and by those whose footprints carry you home to where you belong.

♦ ♦ ♦

May your fears come gently knocking at your door.

♦ ♦ ♦

Of all the patterns that cross familial generations, love is indeed the greatest.

♦ ♦ ♦

Even if you plant yourself in one place, you have the power to bloom everywhere.

♦ ♦ ♦

Don't let powerlessness overcome you. Allow it to mold you into the gentle warrior that understands it as a pathway to inner strength.

♦ ♦ ♦

The temptation to heal is far greater than the temptation to stay wounded. Sometimes we forget that.

♦ ♦ ♦

The person you become when you fail at something might just teach you more about yourself than the person you are when you easily succeed.

♦ ♦ ♦

How magnificent are those weaknesses that teach you to befriend yourself with kindness.

◆ ◆ ◆

I know many of us are frightened by the pause.

That singular moment when the door between inner peace and inner chaos compels us to make a choice to grasp stillness in its entirety or walk through that door facing the unknown.

That singular moment where the possibility of new life can be birthed by our co-creation with the Divine.

Or that moment, yes, that moment, where we meet death in its many forms, staring into our souls, wondering what our next move will be.

I know many of us are frightened by the pause.

That space inside of us where emotion and thought can have no comprehensible boundary and wreak havoc with how we see ourselves in this world.

That space inside of us that is so quiet we can hear the screams of our ancestors and those who will walk the path for us in the future.

Or perhaps that space where our sense of being is destined by the gods in ways we don't understand yet, and in knowing so, we become fearful of trusting.

I know many of us are frightened by that pause. That pause has helped me navigate these life-giving waters; these thoughts and emotions rippled with currents of the Divine.

Without it, life would not exist as we know it.

Embrace the pause. Respect the pause.

Pray for that pause to find you even when you cannot find it within yourself.

✦ ✦ ✦

Show me your weakness and I will show you the stuff legends are made of.

✦ ✦ ✦

Gather yourself slowly.
Until you hear the voice of God whispering in your ear, "Everything is going to be okay."

✦ ✦ ✦

Grow your tribe. One seed at a time.

✦ ✦ ✦

Don't slay the dragon. Become one with it. By understanding its true nature, you begin to understand part of your own.

✦ ✦ ✦

That which frightens you might ultimately illuminate you.

✦ ✦ ✦

There is that one pivotal moment before you surrender when you look back at the darkness and wonder if you should stay because it is so familiar. Some might tremble with uncertainty, others might exhale in anticipation of freedom. We all come to that place every day in our lives. These choices are not always easy, but rest assured we are always held in those moments.

✦ ✦ ✦

Our vulnerabilities are ours to honor, not another's to judge.

✦ ✦ ✦

To behold such beauty in this world, one would have to find it in himself first.

✦ ✦ ✦

The silence cannot hear you if you keep talking.

♦ ♦ ♦

When the "rules" of your life suddenly change, don't look to change your life. Look to change yourself.

♦ ♦ ♦

May we tread so humbly on the earth that not even the trees notice our footprints.

♦ ♦ ♦

Bear witness to your vulnerability ever so gently so that you walk the path with more strength than you could ever imagine.

♦ ♦ ♦

You cannot find yourself until you become aware that you are lost.

♦ ♦ ♦

You are greater than your unworthiness. If you refuse to believe that, then you will never feel like you are enough.

♦ ♦ ♦

May there be days when my wind remains strengthened by the light that even the darkest of hurricanes recedes in my presence.

♦ ♦ ♦

Don't just stop and smell the roses. Become one.

♦ ♦ ♦

The undoing of something can take lifetimes. Let us be mindful of creating a world based on fear.

♦ ♦ ♦

There is a place beyond words. Meet me there so we may sit in the silence together.

◆ ◆ ◆

The longing to know yourself will cease when the need to self-judge no longer has a place in your existence.

◆ ◆ ◆

There are times I want to be the storm after the calm; the one in which my restlessness battles surrender, feeling every nuance of purification as it seeps into my weary bones, knowing the phoenix will rise when the time comes as called forth by the heavens. Being as present as I can with emotions as raw as thunder and lightning. Watching them become one with the skies and the earth, as my heart and mind endeavor to survive a reality which at any moment will no longer exist. There are times I want to be the storm after the calm, seduced by the inner and outer turbulence of the Divine as it shifts me, knowing in the end that the self I thought I knew will be even closer in alignment to the heavens once this storm has passed.

◆ ◆ ◆

True freedom is bound by holiness.
Humbly honor those who have fallen
So we may endeavor to rise.

◆ ◆ ◆

I need me first before I can need you.

5

BALANCE

The moon will teach you what you are afraid to learn from the sun.

◆ ◆ ◆

Our medicine cannot be found through illusion. Look for it amidst the living things of this world, its peoples, its plants, its trees, its rocks. Look for it amidst the footprints of your neighbors, no matter how different they appear to you. Look for it in the manifestations of the Divine in the clouds and the stars. Our medicine will be that which connects us all and renders us as equals under the Creator. Our medicine will be that which is above all else and teaches us about love.

◆ ◆ ◆

All darkness and all light is simply illusion. It presents itself in the way that it does to serve the greater purpose of coordinating universal and natural law. It serves an even greater purpose in helping human beings to identify their scope of consciousness and their responsibilities that lie therein. In the beginning, there was silence. And in that silence, the light and the darkness were born. Within those polarities, many dimensions came into existence and experience. We, as human and spiritual beings, have been created to learn within these existences and experiences.

Without the understanding of the light of God that we hold and our own inner darkness, we cannot come to know God within ourselves, one another, or the world. When we ask the question as to why evil exists, we will usually look toward the heavens for answers. It is far easier to look externally than to face the truth by looking deeply within ourselves. When we become aware of what evil truly is as the way God intended it, we will begin to face it with the courage and perspective that is needed for emotional and spiritual growth. It has been said in many a tradition that God will not give to you more evil than you can handle. So how in this statement can we affirm our belief in a loving Creator, especially during these challenging times?

We can begin to understand by grasping the concept of evil as relative to the light of God, as opposed to the structure of evil that is created by the will of man. When we separate ourselves from evil, then we are not embracing all aspects of our soul. Evil was meant to be placed in perspective and respect of the light of God—a necessary means for our understanding of truth. Evil can rest in stillness and fear of the spiritual process that surrounds Divine Providence. Whether it is the light or the darkness, good or evil, all energies need to be in stillness for the energy of God to come forth. If an energy is not in stillness, then it will leave itself open to the spiritual laws as set forth by the universe.

All souls have a learning continuum that reflects the accumulation of experiences collectively and universally. Light is born from light, and darkness is born from darkness. The same holds true for the antithesis. Darkness must also be born from light, and light must also be born from darkness so that the spiral continues. The universal truths must come into balance within those polarities. Each polarity yields the grace, mercy, forgiveness, and appropriate boundaries to hold space for the other to come into balance. That is why one can and needs to be born unto the other.

Each person on his or her own path looks toward God for truth and understanding. The spiritual process that we each face encourages the formation of universal thoughts and attitudes that help to reflect the state of consciousness we are in universally. As we embrace the light, we reflect it. As we embrace the darkness, we reflect that as well. As we learn to balance the two, we assist in the universal balance that is in alignment with the will of God. Part of the natural evolution of our human psychology is and has always been to interpret the light and the darkness mentally, emotionally, and physically. We see and know these paradigms through the experiences of our emotional body and then tend to intellectualize our reactions to them instead of seeing and perceiving them in truth and reality. Where do we confuse truth and reality with our perceptions? Everywhere except within that space when we are in stillness with God. For each person, that space unfolds uniquely.

◆ ◆ ◆

One day the women will rise in both worlds and give birth to a new generation of thinkers. Until then, may we be given the strength to forgive them their trespasses; for those who do not have the courage to honor a woman and her rights will one day walk behind her in humility.

◆ ◆ ◆

The nature of your service to the Creator can be redefined at any moment of your awakening.

◆ ◆ ◆

If you wait too long for the hero to appear on your journey, you miss the chance of getting to know yourself.

◆ ◆ ◆

If you can stand in the silence for a few moments, you will hear every heartbeat of those who came before you. If you can stand in the silence a while longer, you just might hear the heartbeats of those yet to be born. If you allow yourself to become one with the silence, your heartbeat will live on forever, merging with every soul, past and present, until every heart beats as one.

◆ ◆ ◆

You cannot see the sunlight if all you are being shown is the darkness.

◆ ◆ ◆

I became aware of my strength the moment I accepted my weaknesses.

◆ ◆ ◆

There are those who surrender to gratitude.

Who understand truths within humanity that breathe life into their souls.

Who speak softly of the Divine, from which many blessings stream forth into this wayward world.

There are those who surrender to gratitude.

Who understand the effortlessness of the Divine to give life with all its challenges, heartache, grief, and wickedness, raw with emotion that overwhelms humanity.

Life can be taken as easily as it is given. Joy and happiness seem fleeting but lie abundantly within the silence, within the grace, within the effortlessness.

Blessings may not be easily seen or heard, felt or experienced, but are imbued powerfully by the Holy Spirit.

And for those whose faith is embodied, that surrender is steadfast.

There are those who surrender to gratitude.

Bitterness does not take hold of their spirits.

Their gratitude flows freely between the heavens and the earth, between all kingdoms under Creation, abiding by those spiritual laws at work.

Appreciating the task at hand to love thy brethren with their whole heart and soul, to love the earth as much as the womb that carried them between worlds.

There are those who do not know how to surrender.

Who hold tightly to fear, to doubt, to the uncertainty that plagues human hearts.

To the abandonment of self within our wayward world.

To the abandonment of self within the cosmos.

To the abandonment of self within Godnature.

There are those who do not know how to surrender as they do not yet understand gratitude.

It lies within them, a palpable force to be reckoned with, a sense of unyielding freedom from all attachment and desire.

From what is past, what is present, and what is yet to come.

There are those who fear gratitude, the unknown that comes with it, the perceived sense of powerlessness.

May we join together within God's sanctity, within a moment of silence, to understand the immense beauty that is shared for a life worth being grateful for.

A life that is our own, one that is another's, and for those lives that walk within every dimension between the heavens and the earth.

◆ ◆ ◆

The river will flow in your direction once you learn to respect its nature. It cannot be forced but is influenced in response to your humility and appreciation for its life-giving energies.

◆ ◆ ◆

Blessed are the imperfections that keep us humble.

◆ ◆ ◆

An experience of presence during a moment of solitude will remind you of who you truly are.

◆ ◆ ◆

It's the way you hold your darkness that matters. Pretending it doesn't exist within you is futile.

◆ ◆ ◆

Become inspired by your own willingness to grow.

◆ ◆ ◆

That in-between place that you're just not quite sure is considered holy ground. Your healing medicine awaits you.

◆ ◆ ◆

Seek shelter in those places that have forgotten how to dwell in holiness. You will find them waiting where you once left them.

◆ ◆ ◆

That within you that feels so unwanted perhaps awaits your gentle hand in a friendship that will last an eternity.

◆ ◆ ◆

I have questioned the existence of God when not once has She questioned mine. A faith embodied breathes life into your soul.

◆ ◆ ◆

You cannot climb the mountain without coming to know yourself in the process.

◆ ◆ ◆

I become increasingly inspired by our potential to love unconditionally.

◆ ◆ ◆

Compassion enriches the soul, whereas pity renders it helpless.

◆ ◆ ◆

Fall into silence gracefully until you no longer see yourself as separate.

◆ ◆ ◆

Gather yourself slowly so you become acquainted with all those parts of yourself you were afraid to love.

◆ ◆ ◆

One day the masculine and feminine will rise in unity, remembering they were born both of the same wound and the same love.

◆ ◆ ◆

Become the path.

◆ ◆ ◆

Life doesn't pass you by. It walks beside you until you take notice of just how integral a part you play in its direction.

◆ ◆ ◆

Lay your footprints gently on the earth, much in the same way you desire the clouds to carry your prayers to the heavens. We cannot treat one world with such blatant disregard while expecting the other to consecrate us.

◆ ◆ ◆

An elder doesn't show you the path. He shows you your strength so you can walk the path.

◆ ◆ ◆

Become the shelter you seek.

◆ ◆ ◆

Falling from grace is easy. Picking yourself back up is all about choice.

◆ ◆ ◆

Return to the sacred as though you never left.

◆ ◆ ◆

Your deepest wound might just be your greatest blessing.

◆ ◆ ◆

If you don't like your life, change your perception of it.

◆ ◆ ◆

All emotions are gateways to another realm. They are not your final destination.

◆ ◆ ◆

You cannot rush to the other side of powerlessness.

It is a deep void embedded into the unknown of human constructs, serving many thoughts and emotions that have the potential of leading us into the darkness.

We spend much of our lives individually and collectively searching for, attaching to, utilizing, and manipulating power.

That doesn't necessarily have to be a negative thing; it all depends on our relationship to power itself and how we sit inside ourselves when we are without it—powerless. It is a void many of us prefer not to spend too much time in, albeit a necessary construct for appropriate psychological, emotional, and spiritual development. Our lives are predicated on an energy that has both the power to heal and to destroy. In my experience, rushing through to the other side of powerlessness to find empowerment leads me nowhere. Empowerment is not something one can find. It is a birthright as much as powerlessness is. Sit inside your powerlessness as much as you want to sit inside your power. One cannot exist without the other. Nor will your life be defined any differently as you experience both polarities, dependent on your relationship to them.

◆ ◆ ◆

Our attachment to power will always circle back to help us right the wrongs we have done when we have overstepped its bounds.

◆ ◆ ◆

Glory finds itself amidst the humble.

◆ ◆ ◆

Rest gently in the unknown and you shall never be lost.

◆ ◆ ◆

Conquer what lies within you before you conquer what lies ahead.

◆ ◆ ◆

When your childhood wounds rise up to meet you, receive them gently. May you remind them of their innocence before the pain.

◆ ◆ ◆

The light is not at the end of the tunnel. It *is* the tunnel.

◆ ◆ ◆

Honor the sacred before you lose yourself to that which is unholy.

◆ ◆ ◆

"Meet me halfway," God whispered.
"Where do I begin?" I asked.

"At the threshold of your holiness.
The very moment you were conceived.
The abode of my silent heart."

"I'm not sure where that is.
I'm not sure I trust you."

"I trust you," God said lovingly.
"My soul has faith in yours.
You begin where you feel safest.
The abode of your own heart.
There I will wait for you.
An eternity, when you are ready."

◆ ◆ ◆

Self-nurturing begins when we allow the Divine to touch us at the very core of our womb—that holy place where innocence meets vulnerability.

◆ ◆ ◆

Don't confuse inner reflection with self-judgment.

◆ ◆ ◆

Let today be the day your relationship to your own inadequacy changes and you begin to remember the light of your own being.

♦ ♦ ♦

When I speak with those beyond the veil, they are sometimes confounded by those of us here who have forgotten how to live.

♦ ♦ ♦

A heart unattended will lead to misery.
A mind unattended will lead to doubt.
A soul unattended will lead to chaos.

♦ ♦ ♦

May your innocence encourage you to walk through Divine Darkness knowing any emptiness you feel will be replenished by God's grace.

♦ ♦ ♦

Anyone can show you the path, but it is yours to walk.

♦ ♦ ♦

Don't be afraid to slay the dragon. It is only as big as you think it is.

♦ ♦ ♦

Faith can spread like wildfire in the most vulnerable of spaces, leaving you destined to follow the path of your heart and not the misgivings of your mind.

♦ ♦ ♦

Our tendency to overanalyze any darkness that comes our way will give it more power over us than the gods intended.

♦ ♦ ♦

It has been said that with determination "one can move mountains." It was only when I learned to respect those mountains that I was afforded the privilege of moving *with* them.

◆ ◆ ◆

When in doubt, seek stillness over movement. You will find it takes much less effort and offers greater reward.

◆ ◆ ◆

To have a profound life one must engage in the simplicity of being.

◆ ◆ ◆

Your anger is not the issue. Your relationship to it is.

◆ ◆ ◆

I remember when God molded me in my weakness, as that was what led me to find where my true strength came from.

◆ ◆ ◆

You don't have to wait for the ashes to rise.

Rise from the ashes because you know you can. Not because it is something you think you have to do!

◆ ◆ ◆

May you find substance in your inner work before you suffer needlessly.

◆ ◆ ◆

There comes a time when our existential experiences no longer fulfill a destiny we thought we were aligned with.

Our perception of the Divine shifts as our lives unfold into realities we don't quite understand, realities that no longer serve a purpose and have carried us thus far.

We will seek illumination amidst the mundane, transformation amidst the darkness, stillness amidst that which unsettles us, revelation amidst the unknown.

◆ ◆ ◆

May your unworthiness inspire you to do great things.

◆ ◆ ◆

The journey home begins when you remember you never really left.

◆ ◆ ◆

Before you slay the dragon in front of you, slay the one that lives inside of you.

◆ ◆ ◆

Quiet the desperation that prevents you from feeling secure in the unknown.

◆ ◆ ◆

At the threshold of illusion, you will have the choice to bear witness to the Beloved or stay in the perplexities of your own making.

◆ ◆ ◆

Go deep into the stillness and you will find your way home.

◆ ◆ ◆

The brave dare to see the light in others. Meanwhile, the faint of heart seek out the darkness.

◆ ◆ ◆

Wherever you flow in the river of life, I will meet you there.

◆ ◆ ◆

When you finally speak from the heart;
the trees will stand still,
the winds will calm,
the sun will burn brightly,
the birds will sing melodiously,
the earth will listen for your voice,
and the Divine will know you by your name.

◆ ◆ ◆

Live your prayer so passionately that the heavens can't help but dance to your rhythm.

◆ ◆ ◆

You have found your path once you quiet the need to continually search for it. It is not always where you think it is. It might even be in that space where you have least likely looked. The intense attachment we have to defining the right road for us sometimes obscures the very ground we have been standing on all along.

◆ ◆ ◆

We always have a choice to feel empowered at that very moment we feel powerless.

◆ ◆ ◆

The most abundant human resource we have in our midst is love.

◆ ◆ ◆

Even when you stop praying, God listens for the sound of your voice.

◆ ◆ ◆

The true measure of self-love is when you can love yourself in your own silence.

◆ ◆ ◆

You can't rush what God slows down.

◆ ◆ ◆

Where every animal teaches earth medicine,
    we become one with God.

◆ ◆ ◆

When your world turns upside down, turn with it. What you
see as struggle might just be your pathway to peace.

◆ ◆ ◆

Grief molded by solemnity yields rebirth.

◆ ◆ ◆

Lightness of mind yields lightness of heart.

◆ ◆ ◆

Tell your story to the mountains.
Tell your story to the trees.
Tell your story to the winds.
Tell your story to the clouds.
Share your dreams with the stars.
Share your dreams with the moon.
Share your dreams with the sun.
Share your dreams with the earth.
Your story belongs to all Creation.
Your dreams belong to the Divine.
Tell your story, they will listen.
Share your dreams, they will believe.
One voice, one vision, one God.

◆ ◆ ◆

Praying grounds your soul with God's.

♦ ♦ ♦

The slower you walk in your shadow, the more gracious you will be of your light when you come upon it.

♦ ♦ ♦

The mystic does not seek knowledge.
He seeks silence in all Creation.
She seeks splendor in all humanity.
He seeks the mystical within himself.
She seeks the profound within others.
Knowledge without stillness: an incomplete journey.

♦ ♦ ♦

The act of self-discipline becomes easier the moment we let go of the illusions we have about ourselves.

♦ ♦ ♦

Find God sitting on the mountaintop.
Find God listening to the winds.
Find God gathering nourishment for Creation.
Find God dancing with the stars.
Find God singing with the moon.
Find God praying with the sun.
Find God healing with the rain.
Find God smiling with the birds.
Find God playing with His children.
Find God calling you back home.

♦ ♦ ♦

Your own holiness can move mountains.

♦ ♦ ♦

Your inner freedom once realized is a choice, and that is only after one recognizes it as a gift.

♦ ♦ ♦

The storm will pass more easily when you no longer see it as a storm.

♦ ♦ ♦

In between ego and awareness is where you will find your inner warrior.

♦ ♦ ♦

Friends who truly listen value both your words and your silence.

♦ ♦ ♦

Walk mindfully amid the haste and the parallel universes will unveil themselves to you.

♦ ♦ ♦

You morphed from what you thought you should be into a greater awareness of self, that which love knew you already to be. And from there, you continued to be molded into a form that is eternally formless in both mind and spirit. The version of you once a mere spark of existence sought to become one with the entirety of the universe. You no longer look back at your prior existence; why should you?

♦ ♦ ♦

Not a day goes by that the sun doesn't rise with the unbearable effulgence of its own existence.

And when it sets, it recalls effortlessly the honor bestowed on it to play such a significant role in Creation.

If only humans were to value all of life in that way.

♦ ♦ ♦

A wise man speaks his truth. An enlightened one lives it.

♦ ♦ ♦

Both the sun and the moon were needed to help define the purpose of the sky. When the sky finally realized that, she stopped comparing the two and saw how both could exist in support of her journey, how each balanced the other and was necessary for her continued evolution.

What appeared to be an illusion manifested as truth.

♦ ♦ ♦

Somewhere in the midst of the emptiness you will find yourself, I promise.

♦ ♦ ♦

The alteration of humanity is deemed sacred by the gods. Your inherent holiness remains unscathed. What is being altered is how you carry yourself and others within that holiness. Touch upon it gently and you will never know fear again.

♦ ♦ ♦

Sometimes the loneliest place is that pivotal moment when you lose sight of your inner strength.

Forged from grace, that strength is insurmountable by any illusion of fear that comes your way.

♦ ♦ ♦

The chance to dream is bestowed upon those who believe that dreams are powerful prayers that rise above our illusions.

♦ ♦ ♦

From God's heart we are birthed into our mother's womb, destined to embody grace incarnate.

◆ ◆ ◆

God said, "Let there be light."

And with that, the darkness descended.

And all Her children panicked with dread.

Fearing the worst for humankind, they isolated themselves, spread hysteria, ridiculed pariahs, believed in untruths until reality became so obscure they could no longer see who they were amidst the darkness.

God watched Her children, confounded by their lack of faith and understanding.

"I said let there be light," God stated emphatically to Her children.

"The darkness is only a construct within the light for you to see yourselves and those relationships you have with others clearly.

"Your fear only makes it greater. If you truly believe that all was created in my image and likeness, then believe that within every darkness there is a purpose: one so great that your worst fears are hindering any possibility for you to understand the truths about Creation, or even the truths about your own realities. You have the choice to see things differently."

◆ ◆ ◆

To My Yearning Heart

When you think you have banished all thoughts and traces of hope, therein will lie the darkness of all your maladies. What is it that you fear? Do not overlook the fact that the wisdom bestowed upon you to obtain your heart's truest desires shall always reign truth within the Universe. When you seek to know true love and splendor, righteousness has no place amidst the humility of the heart. Can you not see the soul when you look into your lover's eyes? That's right. I am speaking about your own reflection. Look at yourself in the mirror. Behold the beauty that you are. You and your lover are one. Your lover may be your mother, your child, your friend, your soul mate. Your lover is the air you breathe, the shadow that follows you, the earth you rest your weary feet on, the sun whose light embraces your own. When you seek to understand your lover's grievances against you, do not overshadow his or her fears with your presumptions. *If you cannot grant another peace, how is it, dear heart, that you can create a space for your own?*

The universe will present each one of us with a gift: the responsibility to love for the greater good of the person we meet on our path. With that responsibility comes power, and with that power comes choice. If you walk in the light you will head closer to me, your soul. Each time you falter, you will enter into the darkness, but I will still be there waiting for you. You will not know it, though. You will yearn for me. The sanctity of your agreement with me will incite your search to find the light, to find me. To find me, we will start at the beginning again. We will start at love. I will ask you to cherish me. I will ask you to sacrifice. I will ask you to redeem yourself of your holiest virtues. I will ask you to stare into your lover's eyes and to let go of what you presume to know about love. I will ask you to let go of yourself.

I will walk with you hand and hand as we begin again. We will learn together that opportunity arises as true sacrifice yields humility and grace. Heart, you are not individual. I will help you to go beyond your understanding, past the self-grandeur, past the ego, and into the heart of another, into the soul of another, into the soul of yourself.

Why, you ask? Why not.

You will encounter a selfless bliss embraced by the totality of two that are joined as one. Your mind will become incoherent of any untruth that your ego sets before you. Your aspirations of aligning with the Divine will be much easier once I am with you. The need to interfere or control love will no longer have power over you. You and I will become lovers. Isn't that what you have always wanted?

My dear Heart, I wait for you in the unknowing. I wait for you in the uncertainty. I am at peace waiting. I know one thing. You are not at peace waiting until you join me.

Much Love,
Your Soul

6

RECONCILIATION

I don't want to outgrow my fear. I want to sit with it quietly and let it teach me all those things about myself I was afraid to learn. And maybe one day, perhaps, it will outgrow me, and our relationship will evolve into a beautiful friendship.

◆ ◆ ◆

The ground beneath us becomes holy not by the color of our skin or religion we follow. It becomes holy by the intentions our footprints lay for *all* life that has walked the earth—the past, the present, and the future. Embracing the two-leggeds and the four-leggeds and those with wings who hover between the worlds.

◆ ◆ ◆

True gratitude is not fleeting; it is omnipresent.

◆ ◆ ◆

Bear witness to your own unworthiness and you will have opened a door to cultivating self-love.

◆ ◆ ◆

Define me by your projections and it will only make me stronger. Your fears compel me to conquer my own.

Your anger pushes me to forgive myself and those who have hurt me.

Your loneliness helps me befriend my own with kindness.

Your bitterness incites me to appreciate life more than you could imagine.

Your callousness only reminds me that all of life is sacred.

Define me by your projections and you will have only succeeded in creating more anguish for the reality you exist within.

Thank you for reminding me just how strong I truly am.

♦ ♦ ♦

I Stand Next to You

I stand next to you, tired and weary, embracing a Bible, yet you still look to Me for hope.

I stand next to you, empty, opening Myself to you, embracing a Torah, yet you remain hopeless.

I stand next to you, with the greatest of faith in your soul, embracing the Koran, yet you no longer look My way.

I stand next to you, with fervent prayer for your well-being, embracing the Kangyur or one of the texts from the Chinese Buddhist Canon, yet you do not trust Me anymore.

I stand next to you, imploring your forgiveness, not just for Me but for yourself and your brethren. I am embracing the Bhagavad-Gita, yet forgiveness is nowhere to be found.

I stand next to you, loving you, with the hope that you will love Me back. I am embracing the Guru Granth Sahib.

I stand next to you always even though you continue to seek Me out. You cannot see Me if you cannot see Me in others. If you cannot see Me in others, you cannot see Me in yourself. I am your God, I am your Goddess, I am the Divine. Continue to judge Me by the Scriptures I embrace and you have failed at one of my greatest teachings; to love thy neighbor as thyself. The Scriptures do not frighten you. The children embracing those Scriptures do not frighten you. You frighten yourself because of the realization that you are loved so intensely by Me and by those you call your enemies.

Put down your judgment. Embrace the Bible as much as the Torah. Respect the Koran as much as the Bhagavad Gita. Go beyond the form. Then and only then will you see Me embracing you. Then and only then will you feel the faith I have for you. Then and only then will you trust Me. And only then will you forgive Me, and in doing so, you will forgive yourself.

I wait patiently.

◆ ◆ ◆

You know that saying,
    "When God closes one door, She opens another."
    Those words have become jaded over time, and I needed a little more from God.
    So one day, I asked Her to elaborate.
    She didn't speak to me in words, but instead showed me pictures in my mind.
    The blueprints for my special door, well, She laid them out months in advance.
    With painstaking effort, She would rummage through dimensions in Her mind.
    She wanted the right size to carry all of me through it. My heart, my soul, my body.
    My fears, my pain, my joys, my every happiness.

It had to be the right hue of the rainbow, a color that would embrace my every light and comfort my every darkness.

She wanted to make sure I knew completely that my special door was never shut, only those doors in my mind were.

She even laid out the red carpet and adorned it with all of my favorite things.

She was so excited that She placed the door in a spot where I would always see it and waited for me with open arms to walk through it whenever I needed to.

You know that old saying.

Well, I don't need it anymore.

God built me a door, the greatest door I could ever ask for.

She actually built one for everyone.

◆ ◆ ◆

May we cherish our vulnerabilities as much as we contain our power. May we never forget the beauty we carry as women and pass that on to future generations with a reverence unparalleled in times past. In honor of the feminine, may we endeavor to rise in our holiness.

◆ ◆ ◆

Give someone an ounce of hope and you just opened up his or her world. And in doing so, you just opened up your own.

◆ ◆ ◆

Intimacy happens when you nurture an aspect of self you never knew existed while uncovering the truth of who you really are.

◆ ◆ ◆

Across generations, you will come to know me. I am your past, your present, your future. I belong to those who were left behind by the constructs of linear time, yet exist in parallel realities where

I can touch upon you the imprint of my soul. You think you exist in your world without me. You think I can exist without you. You think we can exist without each other. You look in the mirror and define yourself by the present awareness of your human condition yet fail to realize you are merely a thread weaving through the conscience of immortality. Today you might experience yourself as man or woman. Yesterday you were in my womb, in utero, waiting to be born. Nourished by the same placenta that fed you for generations before. Who will you be in this lifetime?

Do you remember who we were in other lifetimes? Were you the slave, shackled and haunted by his owner until you were weary to the bone from working his plantations? Or were you the plantation owner, filled with the undeniable assurance that I was merely property for you to own? Were you Cherokee (among others) leaving your lands, malnourished and broken from walking the Trail of Tears? Or were you the militia pointing the gun in my back as I took my last steps, not able to feel the ground underneath my feet anymore. Were you a woman desperate to end an unwanted pregnancy with a back-alley abortion or the person that fought against equal rights for women? Or were you perhaps the child that never came to term? Or maybe the child working twelve-hour shifts in a city factory before child labor laws were enacted to protect you. Or maybe you were the factory boss, walking around intimidating me, knowing that what little monies I received for my intense labor would not be sufficient to help my family. Perhaps you were a physician in the early part of the twentieth century. Or perhaps you were one of the patients turned away because of the color of your skin when hospitals were segregated.

Perhaps across generations you will come to understand that my wound is your wound and your wound is mine. Perhaps you will come to understand that how you live your life will impact mine and all of us you are connected with beyond the veil. Perhaps you will come to understand that the choices you make will impact generations to come, and you, like me, will be watching from a distance. Perhaps.

◆ ◆ ◆

Rebirth yourself into holiness, one so profound that your experience of self is intertwined with another, and another, and another. Until you come to the realization that your journey is one you never walk alone. Embraced by every grief and every joy in the conscience of Creation, your experience only magnifies that which was already born of light. It only took you this long to accept it.

◆ ◆ ◆

Our feelings of inadequacy can feel overwhelming and propel us into a state of powerlessness. We feel as if we have no control over who or what we are or who or what others perceive us to be. It is an addictive emotional spiral that takes us down the rabbit hole searching for something that has actually never left us. Beyond the shame, beyond the loss, beyond the powerlessness, there is an identity that has yet to be discovered within ourselves.

◆ ◆ ◆

Meet your inadequacy with reverence, as it will give you the opportunity to go deeper into yourself with the love that is needed.

◆ ◆ ◆

The path will rise up to meet you once you stop searching for it.

◆ ◆ ◆

Plant seeds that will heal the wounds of those beyond the veil, and you will begin to see your own life change.

◆ ◆ ◆

How great it is to succumb to failure with such a profound sense of worthiness that your spirit knows nothing but inner peace.

♦ ♦ ♦

The earth will carry our bitterness for a very short time until it beckons us to realize we are not the only living manifestations of God's love.

♦ ♦ ♦

The unknown is the new safe. Befriend it so you suffer less.

♦ ♦ ♦

Seek shelter within your own home.
The one God built for you to know love.

♦ ♦ ♦

When you can find yourself in the darkness, that is when you know you never lost your light.

♦ ♦ ♦

I want to be in attendance during my own awakening.

Feet gently touching the earth, feeling her capacity to carry me through my journey. Emotions raw and encapsulated by a collective conscience I have yet to fully comprehend.

♦ ♦ ♦

May your sorrows be lifted by those whose footprints walk beside yours. Gather your holiness and be sheltered by those beyond the veil; those who walk beside you, in front of you, behind you. Even though you cannot see them, even though you cannot hear them, your holiness calls to them, and their holiness calls to you. The veil is thin, and they are near. Reach within and touch your holiness, and you will be touching their spirit upon yours.

♦ ♦ ♦

When unworthiness finds its way to you, bless it as your teacher, and let no harm come to others because of it.

♦ ♦ ♦

There will come a time when one language will be spoken on this earth.

The two-leggeds and the four-leggeds will speak the same tongue.

The trees will share the same voice as humankind.

The mountains and rocks will call you by your name.

The waters will speak through you and to you, and you through them.

There will come a time when one language will be spoken on this earth.

Man, woman, animal, and nature will speak the same words as the heavens.

One language.

One Creation.

♦ ♦ ♦

There are only so many ways we can continue to separate ourselves within humanity. Individuation will eventually lead us into the darkness when we neglect the collective being, the collective soul, the collective heart, and the collective mind. We have moved into a paradigm where the collective soul is made manifest through every thought, action, intention, and service. This paradigm is no longer a choice, as we are being propelled to move into Presence as opposed to distancing ourselves. Separation will engage us with suffering. Presence will inspire healing.

♦ ♦ ♦

It becomes easier to judge another person's suffering when you find it difficult to create a relationship with your own.

Before you offer someone comfort from their vulnerabilities, make sure it is not you who is needing the comfort in bearing witness to them.

◆ ◆ ◆

We always have a choice to feel empowered at that very moment we feel powerless.

◆ ◆ ◆

If you want to redefine your destiny and those of your children, look to your past and speak with your ancestors. Encourage them to see things differently and your own visions will begin to change.

◆ ◆ ◆

Your story is a culmination of a myriad of stories whose words embody your very purpose in this life experience.

Honor the story with gentleness and understanding, faith and hope, reverence and trust that your story *will* be shared not only by you but by future generations to come. It can never remain hidden in the universe, for you were woven into the threshold of humanity even before you came into this world. So for those who feel their voices might never be heard, know that even a whisper is held in sanctity by those beyond the veil. You are heard, you are held, you are carried from this world to the next and beyond. Your story matters to those who lived generations before you and to those waiting to be born.

◆ ◆ ◆

My desire for solitude is about nurturing me, not rejecting you.
Don't confuse my needs with your wounds.

◆ ◆ ◆

Our stories can be told in a myriad of ways besides the use of words.

Language of memory speaks through thoughts, behavior, cells, blood, tissue, bone.

Our primordial language is not one of words. It reaches above the stratosphere and down into the depths of cellular memory where our ancestral histories dwell.

Speak without words. Listen within the silence.

◆ ◆ ◆

Cellular Memory

I remember twenty-three years ago walking into my chiropractor's office to find a very elderly woman lying prone on one of the tables waiting to receive an adjustment. My chiropractor asked if I would work a little with her. Not knowing why, I approached the frail woman, whose deep brown, sunken eyes still had sparkle, and asked her her name. Back then I did a lot of various hands-on therapies along with my medical intuition work—I actually loved palpating the myriad of frequencies the body had to offer. It allowed me to fine-tune my skills in sensing cell, tissue, and organ imbalance, as well as various ailments within the body. By the many rhythms, I was able to learn much about the stories the body would offer; the ones very often the client would forget and the ones the client didn't even consciously know about. I recall her sharing with me that she had had headaches for years, ones that caused her to suffer greatly, and she couldn't find a way to control them. I put my hands on her frontal lobe to grasp a sense of what was happening and was taken aback quite shockingly at the story her body wanted to share. I took a deep breath, pulled myself closer to her, and began to see the story of her time in the concentration camp during World War II. I asked her if she had any recollection of her childhood, and she made a small remark about being in a concentration camp and not remembering much. It was clear she had no interest in speaking about it, so I kept my hands on her and let her body show me the story while it helped me to track it throughout her body systems. I saw the sexual trauma and the trauma of others she held in her body. I saw her torment for those family members she lost. I saw some of the friends she kept close. I saw the nightmares, the screaming . . . many other things that I chose myself to forget after her cellular memory gave me a firsthand account. I tracked those stories through her body, actually forgetting that I was still in my chiropractor's office awaiting my adjustment. I tracked her story through her eating disorder when she was a young adult. I tracked it through the stories she held on to of other survivors and victims still held in her tissues. I was twenty-seven years old at the time. I had actually visited Dachau in Germany when I was nineteen years old. But nothing could have prepared me for the collective story her body was sharing with me. I had already been working with clients for a few years by that time, but this was my first experience of cellular memory to the degree in which I was experiencing it, based on a collective trauma not just individuated.

I'm not a scientist by any means, but it is understood that nerve impulses carry messages between cells. It is also believed they are encoded within our ancestral patterning, the field of epigenetics. Our bodies are amazing vessels that house thousands of frequencies belonging to thoughts, emotions, experiences, ancestral histories, even the foods we eat. We also carry those stories of other souls we connect with, as their learning facilitates our learning and vice versa. Cellular memory influences our lives on a daily basis more than we could ever imagine; thus, ancestral patterns and collective patterns influence our very experiences. When clients speak about "cutting cords" or breaking the pattern caused by cellular memory, I tend to see things differently. I would rather make space for the memory to do what it needs to do, to serve us individually or collectively in the way that it needs to serve. There is a part of that memory, even if a traumatic one, that is Divine, just as within every darkness one will find light. A chord doesn't need to be cut. When given the appropriate respect and understanding for why it is there, it will be raised to the light by Divine Will, thus helping to bring healing to any imbalance created within the cellular memory. And when space is created within a cell, more stories will come forward, more memories, cognizant or not, of times past. The body knows.

I stayed with that woman for almost an hour. I can't even recall if I received my adjustment. I do remember that the one thing she kept asking me in addition to helping her with her headaches was to help her find true love, that at her age she had never experienced it. I looked up as a hand from the spirit world touched my shoulder. I knew the woman would cross soon and that she would be granted a far greater love than she could have ever hoped for. I placed my hand on her heart and told her the wish would be granted soon. And with that, her cells heard me. Her tissues heard me. Her organs heard me. Her headache dissolved. Her body, and all the stories and souls connected with it, were being granted a mercy far greater than I had ever witnessed.

◆ ◆ ◆

From the lips of the innocent come the words of the gods. Listen humbly.

◆ ◆ ◆

Blessed is he who understands that cultivating patience with oneself is the root of forgiveness toward others.

◆ ◆ ◆

During those times that light comes your way, rejoice. And in those times that evil comes your way, remember to hold it in a space of detachment and stillness. What remains still in truth cannot harm you and will only return to its source. Evil cannot engage you unless you allow it.

♦ ♦ ♦

Depression for each of us is different, simply because we walk that internal road alone. Many can identify an emptiness along this path. The emptiness in and of itself becomes overpowering, so much so that some cannot feel the hand of God beside them or the love of God within them. How could they? This is what many mystics referred to as the Dark Night of the Soul. Within that emptiness, one's sense of self has no boundary, no way of defining a structure that keeps one psychologically and emotionally safe. Most of the boundary system unwinds to such a degree that confusion arises with every emotion experienced. Every thought and action is questioned, and every life experience is called into interrogation for its authenticity.

When depression ensues as a response to emptiness, people become trapped in their emotional bodies and are at a loss as to how to separate the two. Emptiness and depression, when identified together, take depression to a whole different level.

I am witnessing a great fear around emptiness. From there comes the response that triggers depression or radiates the depression one might have been struggling with already.

This emptiness can be one's greatest strength or one's greatest weakness. It takes fortitude to sit with it patiently and allow for one's sense of self to be vulnerable to purification, to transformation, to evolution.

The hand of God will be within your reach at all times.

Who you thought you were will no longer be. Who you will become will not be known to you at that moment in time and for a while after—that is where gentleness and patience are needed. And for some, that is when isolation is needed.

Isolation does not have to be a negative thing. I refer to it as solitude. Patience, isolation, solitude—they can all be overwhelming and trigger a crisis, for the desire to escape heavy emotions as if they were heavy metals is intense.

For those I am able to hold space. I ask them to figure out what makes them safe in my emptiness. Many times, it is nothing they have ever known before. Together, we try to find safe haven, a new relationship that helps them feel empowered enough to sit gently with their emotions. Once we have created a new boundary, we move forward to exploring the depression. One thing remains constant. Who a person is before an episode of depression will be different afterward (as it affects everyone differently) once they hold the emptiness in a different light. Sometimes the depression propels a person into such a swift transformation that it will take time to gather themselves and integrate fully the new awareness.

The depression might not linger, but the emptiness may. My continued prayer is that you be kind and patient with yourself, gentle with the person you thought you were, with the person you are in this very moment in time, with the person you are on your way to becoming.

◆ ◆ ◆

One cannot know his wound intimately until he decides to lay down his armor.

◆ ◆ ◆

Shelter me from my own storm,

Where ego eclipses all Divine Holiness.
A gentle nudge and I will remember.

◆ ◆ ◆

Our vulnerability is a gift inspired by the Creator so that we may walk this earth embracing humility instead of fearing it.

◆ ◆ ◆

When your perception of love changes, so will your path.

◆ ◆ ◆

Enter into love lightly so you may feel every thread of its holiness upon your beating heart. Let its effulgence awaken your senses until eternity is no longer a dream unfulfilled but a tangible reality in which love becomes you, and you become love.

◆ ◆ ◆

May stillness be your strength.
May silence be your armor.
And may faith be your shield.

◆ ◆ ◆

A lover's quarrel should be between you and yourself first.

◆ ◆ ◆

The mountain I need to climb may appear as a small hill or even a stepping-stone to you. But it's my mountain. How I choose to climb is between me and the Divine. How you choose to interpret my experience is between you and yourself.

◆ ◆ ◆

In the uncertainty, there will be that one moment you will feel the hand of God on your shoulder. It is in that one moment when you actually allow it to happen.

♦ ♦ ♦

Cellular excitement unfolds as thoughts of impending touch between flesh arise from sentient beings.

Neurons flicker with exuberance, awaiting energetically for what will manifest physically in any moment. Thoughts and emotions permeate above and beyond self for something so intricate yet simplified in all its glory as a basic human need.

Something humans take for granted at times. Yet powerful enough to change our world, powerful enough to change our human dynamic, powerful enough to heal and to nourish. Something so merciful that we forget the graces bestowed with each embrace from one being to another. Something so forgiving yet so frightening to many—the thought of a human embrace, the thought of an embrace from any living creation under God. So gentle, so needed.

Be benevolent with your gift to touch children of God in the way that you pray to be held yourself by sacredness. A hug in and of itself is the body's living experience of prayer.

♦ ♦ ♦

Arise from the womb gently, child.
The nourishing waters will baptize you
In all that is seen humanly,
In all that is unseen Divinely.
From the waters to the earth,
You will leave many remarkable imprints.
Some so soft, God will notice.
Others so harsh, you will cry.
Running back to the flowing waters,
To the womb that held you.
But there is no going back.

A new womb awaits you, child.
The waters are nothing you know.
You do not know yourself yet.
The waters will soon rise up.
You will come to know them
As you come into knowing yourself.
This womb will be very different.
You will baptize the nourishing waters.
You will give this womb strength.
You will make the womb holy.
You will make the unseen seen.
No more running toward safe haven.
You will be that safe haven.
You will be that sacred womb.

◆ ◆ ◆

How insignificant our egos are in this vast paradigm of love. How human ignorance still undermines the fact that no matter what body we are born into and all the cultural norms associated with it, we are all interconnected beyond the veil in ways we might never understand.

◆ ◆ ◆

Time is shifting in this world. Resurrection is occurring at levels within our human psyche that are contributing to much of the internal and external chaos we are all experiencing. Use these holy days to bear witness to your prayer, to your life, and to *every* life you come into contact with. The only thing stopping you is yourself, your fear, your unworthiness and your lack of faith. You are loved and held more than you could ever imagine. It is time.

◆ ◆ ◆

Tame the Divine in me and I've lost my way.

◆ ◆ ◆

An ego uncompromised has trouble distinguishing truth from illusion.

◆ ◆ ◆

Within the quietness and comfort of solitude, I find distant memories of the person I thought I was. Remnants of my humanity seeking undiscovered possibilities of creating myself anew. Within the quiet, those possibilities exist, individually and collectively. The memories with which we all identify ourselves no longer carry us to our destinies. They served their purpose when needed. Now, we carry ourselves the rest of the way.

◆ ◆ ◆

One who cultivates wisdom without living in service incites the ego to run a fool's errand.

◆ ◆ ◆

God is my muse, both in my weakness and in my strength.

◆ ◆ ◆

I dream of God only to awaken and find Him everywhere.

◆ ◆ ◆

When you begin to become inspired by your own Divine likeness, God's grace will become a constant companion in the creation of your life.

◆ ◆ ◆

May every facet of your unworthiness incite you to gather all that is sacred within.

♦ ♦ ♦

Gather your holiness and approach another's heart with the same reverence as you would your own.

♦ ♦ ♦

God doesn't care what language you speak or what religion is behind your prayers. God cares that your voice is soft and echoes the vibrant harmonies whispered by the angels who honor us in our differences.

♦ ♦ ♦

When desperation arises, soothe it gently.
Let it hear you whisper softly,
"We are all that is here."
Nothing can frighten you, in truth,
More than your own illusions.
May your gentleness bring forth understanding.
Arising from desperation, wholeness awaits you.

♦ ♦ ♦

We are vulnerable in our fears. We are vulnerable in our anger. We are vulnerable in our capacity to love. We are vulnerable in our capacity to hate. The iniquities of this world challenge us to the bone.

♦ ♦ ♦

May your effulgence illuminate my being
In ways I don't yet understand.

♦ ♦ ♦

Be as passionate about letting go of something as you are to holding on to it.

◆ ◆ ◆

Sorrow will illuminate your inner knowing once you come to the realization that it can serve a higher purpose.

◆ ◆ ◆

Be vulnerable in your awareness of God, and you will come to know yourself in ways unimaginable.

◆ ◆ ◆

The time will come when you will learn not to be afraid of your own being.

◆ ◆ ◆

External chaos will come and go. Internal chaos is a choice.

◆ ◆ ◆

I am not how you see me. I am how you see yourself.

◆ ◆ ◆

Hear me when I cannot speak.
Shelter me when I cannot stand.
Comfort me when I cannot comprehend.
Bless me when I cannot appreciate.
Forgive me when I cannot pray.
Love me when I cannot love.

◆ ◆ ◆

The sun doesn't ask permission to rise, as it already knows its inherent holiness.

◆ ◆ ◆

Sometimes we are in such a rush to make changes in our lives that we can't see the changes our lives are making within us.

◆ ◆ ◆

Meet me in the vast unknown
Where you and I become one
Where love is all there is
Where the wounded are made whole
Where the hopeless are given faith
Where the weak are bestowed courage
Where the lost gently find themselves.

◆ ◆ ◆

Listen to others in the ways you want your own voice to be heard.

◆ ◆ ◆

Blessed are they who see the light within the darkness, the strength within the weak, the truth amidst the lie, the healing within the wounding, the peace beyond the despair, the love amidst the hatred, the hope beyond the hopeless, the forgiveness amidst the unforgiven, and the Divine within all.

◆ ◆ ◆

Absence might make the heart grow fonder, but letting go makes the heart grow deeper.

◆ ◆ ◆

God is giving us a choice today. A choice that can either empower our evolution or continue to diminish the sanctity of our spirits. Each day when we awaken, we are given the opportunity to attach to the light or to the darkness, love or hate, faith or fear, oneness or separation. Suffering and joy become subjective as our realities shift with each moment that presents itself to us. We are free to look at every situation, thought, or emotion in the light or in the darkness. How many people don't realize just how much power and freedom the universe bestows upon us?

◆ ◆ ◆

How many of you have asked how a loving Creator can allow for so many terrible things to happen in the world? How many of you are asking as you read this how a loving Creator can allow so many *wonderful* things to happen in the world?

◆ ◆ ◆

The moment you open your eyes tomorrow, you will have the choice to be free. Free from suffering? No, of course not. But you will be free to define suffering to work in your life differently from how it has in the past, free to enable the suffering to humble itself toward grace. Free to love yourself in the midst of it all, and free to once again believe that in every darkness, there will always be light.

What will your choice be today?

◆ ◆ ◆

The moment I touched the earth,
Flesh upon flesh,
Innocence upon innocence,
She called to me from her womb.
Seeing my pain,
The rawness of my unworthiness,
She enveloped me one breath at a time
Until I could no longer feel myself, a reflection of my woundedness
Until I could feel her
Just her
Stroking my hair, caressing my body,
Soothing me until I no longer felt alone,
Belonging to a part of that womb that has nourished me since I entered this realm.
The Goddess embodied in a place that could sometimes be unholy,

Taking my breath and making it her own,
Reminding me that holiness can be found everywhere I lay my
feet upon the ground, upon her.
Earth to earth.
Child to womb.
Soul to soul.
I love you.

◆ ◆ ◆

A broken heart seeks silence in the most unusual places to mend
itself. It is in this silence where the hands of God carry you until
you feel whole again.

◆ ◆ ◆

A grateful heart lights the path for mercy to follow effortlessly in
its tracks.

◆ ◆ ◆

Any failure looked upon with a modicum of gratitude will yield
hidden treasures.

◆ ◆ ◆

The wounded will remain with us until we remember them by
their names—

Each and every one of them, whose valor runs through our
veins, whose purpose carries our breath, whose life force still
protects us in this realm and beyond the veil.

Those are the names of those who triumph amidst darkness,
whose service above self walks within the threshold of the gods.

Remember them by their names. Harken to their voices.

Their wounds become sanctified with every gratitude that
springs forth from our hearts.

♦ ♦ ♦

You are being stripped of familiar boundaries in every relationship you have with yourself and with others.

Internal and external safety has become obsolete.

The rawness with which you are experiencing life is like nothing many of you have known before.

Structures are disintegrating right before your very eyes.

People are changing and becoming unrecognizable.

You are becoming unrecognizable.

These wounds will change you.

They will change us all.

To be alive during this time, to bear witness to humanity and its involution and subsequent evolution, is challenging.

But you are alive. You have that opportunity to recreate your internal and external boundary system with each passing day.

You have the opportunity to choose your reactions to humanity's upheavals as well as your own.

You have the opportunity to rise.

It won't be easy. There will be much more loss to come,

But you are choosing life.

And right now, this is where life is at

For you, for all of us.

7

CHANGES OF WORLDS

The ancestors have spoken throughout the centuries. I can still hear their melodic voices in the ethers just as clearly as I can hear the whispers of the mountains, trees, waters, sun, moon, and stars. The philosophies of the wise men and women aren't changing. It is we who are changing. The philosophies born eons ago are as true today as they were then. Our interpretations are shifting, as well as our understanding of the world, synchronistically on many levels. To the spirit world, we have been in this intense time of purification. For those of us trying to navigate in this world, the past year has been chaotic, to say the least. What I have witnessed most is a great paradigm shift when it comes to relationship as a whole. Familial dynamics have borne the brunt of these changes, as has how we relate to ourselves. Expand that out into the world and many of us don't seem to recognize ourselves anymore.

I listen often; to family, friends, clients, the earth, and myself. A state of confusion has permeated our thought field because what we are experiencing is such a rapid disintegration of an old existence and comprehension of life into a new one that we can hardly make sense of. Our spiritual, psychological, and physical structures don't carry the same weight as they used to in carrying us through to the next moment. It is creating as much fear as it is confusion. The confusion renders many people helpless and overwhelmed. When we do not recognize who we are in any given moment, we destabilize and don't know how to integrate and incorporate any new internal or external structure. How can we? And what about the tools to do so? The ancient wisdom will serve its purpose regardless of our cooperation. I don't care which tradition it flows from. I do care what each of us does with that knowledge.

I still see the ebb and flow where confusion meets stillness. I want to ask all of us to be open to a continually evolving structure on many levels. Let go of what we think it might look like. Yes, it can be very scary to be in the midst of all these changes when it comes to interpersonal relationships. Yes, you possibly won't recognize yourself for a long while, maybe only bits and pieces here and there. Yes, you also may not recognize those closest to you. You may even lose sight of your purpose. What was once familiar may be completely unrecognizable. You might be really afraid to let go. And there will be many times when we are not even sure what to let go of or the direction we are to head in. I think the confusion can serve us if we take the time to let go of all preconceived notions of who we presently are, who we think we should be, and who we want to become. I do believe that some part of our soul already knows the person we are capable of transforming into. The relationships we will enter into, or the new patterns we will enter into with existing relationships, are already waiting for us. This a new period of co-creation. I like to think of it as coming home. I get the fear. I am with you. We are all with you. We are all coming home to ourselves, to each other, and to a natural world that awaits the respect it deserves.

♦ ♦ ♦

Tread lightly upon earth that has already been trampled on. Your footsteps will heal those before you if you walk gently enough.

♦ ♦ ♦

Gather yourself as you walk this sacred earth until the pain of your ancestors is released to the gods. Your story has a frequency that is understood by your ancestors. It will be passed on to your children and their children. The heavens know you by that frequency, as does every living thing in Creation. Learn it. Respect it. Become one with it. Live it, as it will outlive you and be passed on to the degree to which you nurtured its path and evolved with it.

Gather your thoughts until every message that has crossed generations is revealed. Gather your heart until every wound is held in gratitude.

♦ ♦ ♦

May your life become the ceremony your ancestors could only dream of. Make every ritual sacred so that your imprint in both worlds fulfills a destiny you know little of, a destiny that is larger than who you think you are or what your purpose is.

♦ ♦ ♦

Follow me amidst the graves of your ancestors, whose footprints you walk on against the fertile earth beneath you with each passing day. Follow me as my voice beckons, calling out to your mother, your father, your grandmothers and grandfathers, their relations and their relations before them. The earth may carry their bones, but their spirits are ever present in every facet of your being—your anger, your sorrow, your joy, your peace, each emotion permeating every cellular thread from the heavens to the earth. It is between and within those spaces where we have the power to change the past, the present, and the future. When you follow me, you follow every footprint. Your first step, your baby step, your seminal imprint in this world is ensconced within a million footprints. If you want to change the world, honor the footprint. Honor the thread that connects you with a million souls before you and a million souls still awaiting their powerful births into this world. Their stories of creation, their stories of survival, their stories of hope, their stories of love . . . those stories will not change, nor necessarily those that are predestined. What will shift as we honor these footprints is the ways in which we perceive the stories, the ways in which we carry them in our bodies, the ways in which our cellular threads communicate these stories through ancestral genetics. Your ancestors will hear you. Your ancestors will know you differently than they do now. You will come to know.

◆ ◆ ◆

Your inner shaman will awaken when it is you who needs to understand the power of your own soul's medicine.

◆ ◆ ◆

Dedicate your inner work to just one ancestor beyond the veil, and all those in your lineage will rise up and celebrate.

◆ ◆ ◆

Your last thought is not who you are.
Your last emotion is not who you are.
Your last choice is not who you are.
Who you are is how you choose to see yourself in this very present moment.
Thus, choose lovingly.

◆ ◆ ◆

The cumulative rage sweeping across the earth right now requires everyone's participation to be brought into balance. If we don't, we will be lost to its energies in both thought and behavior and the collective human identity will be further unrecognizable. There is a time and a place for every emotion to exist within balance. When it further divides us and incites us to hatred, it will simply continue to redefine a humanistic paradigm built on fear.

◆ ◆ ◆

You will come upon hallowed ground once you understand the sacredness of your own being.

◆ ◆ ◆

She tried so desperately to put her past behind her until she realized her ancestors were the ones paving the way for her destiny to be fulfilled.

◆ ◆ ◆

Weave your memories into a tapestry that you want to remember your life by. You have the choice of which memories you want to hold on to.

◆ ◆ ◆

Secrets held transgenerationally can have a strong influence on the way children form bonds within familial relationships. Core wounds surrounding trust form in utero and can condition a young mind to react and respond to their emotional DNA sometimes when not even understanding where the pattern originates from. The responses and reactions to the long-held secret will actually shift the story behind the secret so that it is told, consciously or not, through the eyes of the new storyteller, a future generation. If you don't want to be bound by the secret or the story, create a new story. Detach from the power the secret has over you. Reintroduce into cellular memory a new response and reaction.

◆ ◆ ◆

Speak to me of a time past, and I will show you the gateway to your future. Not because you reap what you sow, but from a mercy so kind it touches the very soul of your lineage and yearns to be awakened in every footprint on your path. Not as a lesson needing to be completed or something still needing to be learned. Simply because the Divine, through the grace of your ancestors, wants you to know just how much you are loved.

◆ ◆ ◆

A few steps taken in your shoes may be a mile on someone else's path. Judge another by their footsteps and you diminish the integrity of your own.

◆ ◆ ◆

In Your footsteps I will follow
Until Your prayer becomes my prayer,
Until Your sacrifice becomes my sacrifice,
Until Your strength becomes my strength,
Until Your promise becomes my promise.
Until Your Spirit becomes my spirit.
In Your footsteps I will follow
Until You finally call me home.

◆ ◆ ◆

Your encounter with God will be like no other. Savor it.

◆ ◆ ◆

There will come a time when your holiness can do great things. Until then, create a space for your humility to be born.

◆ ◆ ◆

Your identity is based not on what you make of this life but what this life creates within you.

◆ ◆ ◆

Love *your* story. Because if you don't, no one else will.

◆ ◆ ◆

The womb is perhaps the most sacred of portals, where humankind has the privilege of passing from one world into the next.

◆ ◆ ◆

The womb we carry has embraced a thousand souls within, souls that have crossed generations into the world of spirit and those souls that have yet to be born. We do not just carry our own seeds to fertilize; we carry the seeds of many. The child that is born unto us belongs as much to us as it does to each member of the "tribe" we are connected with. We all become mothers, whether or not we actually have children in this lifetime. And we all are given the opportunity to impart the feminine aspects of the Divine in whichever ways we are called to serve. We all share the same mother, through lineages, parallel realities, prior incarnations, and the love of the Creator. The Divine Feminine is the most magical evolutionary aspect of the Creator, born to receive both God and Goddess, born to impart both God and Goddess in all realms of existence. We are the Sanctuary on which the Divine rests and then, when called to, pours forth into this wayward world seeds of healing and grace personified. We are truth embodied in Creation.

Beyond the veil, all the mothers in your lineage—whose wombs endured physical, emotional, and spiritual transformation—planted the seed for your arrival long before you were born. It is because of their earthly existence that your

DNA is created from a tapestry of joys, sorrows, life, death, and continual rebirth. You are a part of what transformed this world eons ago, both in the light and in the darkness.

♦ ♦ ♦

You are the manifestation of many prayers by your ancestors who came before you.

♦ ♦ ♦

May God's tender mercies sweeten those dark places
You are afraid to enter.
And when you soon awaken to find you were only dreaming of separation,
You will realize that you needed nothing more than to trust yourself completely,
One heartbeat at a time.
There she stood, in between two worlds, not sure if her life was but a dream or her dream was of a life, one that she has lived many lifetimes, culminating in a nonlinear reality that the heavens had blessed.

♦ ♦ ♦

I am not afraid of death.
It is merely a change of worlds
Where our brokenness has the chance to mend itself.
I am afraid for life,
A life without God.
A life not lived worthy of love is a life not lived at all.

♦ ♦ ♦

Little by little, those pieces of yourself you cannot gather will be cradled by your ancestors until you are ready to walk again. Your distress becomes their opportunity to mend. Your worries become their possibility to hope. Your fears become their chance for redemption. And then the day will come when you are able to walk farther than you ever have, and you will not recognize yourself. The healing that your ancestors have done on your behalf will trickle into your soul like tears of joy from heaven. You will have not only gathered yourself, but all those who rejoice along with you in this time of transformation.

◆ ◆ ◆

The Divine already sees us unclothed. The shadow cannot hide what is already deemed worthy by the light.

◆ ◆ ◆

A mother's prayer opens a portal between the worlds like no other. As she birthed you through the womb, the prayers of her spirit and those of every woman in her lineage graced that womb for your entry into this world.

The bridge connecting yesterday to tomorrow transcends time and space, whereas generations of your ancestors await your healing to make your lineage whole again. There is no time boundary beyond this world. When you smile, they smile. When you cry, they cry. When you love, they love. When you hate, they hate. Your wounds are greater than you alone, as is the ability to move beyond them and partake in transgenerational healing. Staying stuck in pain doesn't allow you to see the whole, the world beyond this one, the world that awaits you and your ancestors as you heal.

◆ ◆ ◆

Children are born not because we willed them to be, but because the Divine wanted to make manifest the continuation of pure love. Raise them in the image of the heavens and not in the image your ego would have. Their souls depend on it. Your soul depends on it, as well those souls who have come before you and those still waiting to be born.

◆ ◆ ◆

The womb is the most miraculous portal created by the hand of God for transient spiritual beings to enter into an earthly world. It bridges one linear reality to the next. It is a resting place between lifetimes. Treat it as you would any other sacred space.

◆ ◆ ◆

Your heart belongs to your ancestors.
Your footprints belong to your ancestors.
Your life belongs to your ancestors.
Your joys belong to your ancestors.
Your sorrows belong to your ancestors.
Praise them as you praise God.
Their stories emanate from the heavens.
And one day, so will yours.

◆ ◆ ◆

Your life connects to many souls.
Embrace their footsteps sacredly within yours.

◆ ◆ ◆

Reincarnation happens when the Divine integrates your soul with another's in various lifetimes so that no soul ever feels untouched or alone. We are all interwoven threads of one another. A soul's notion of being truly alone on their journey is simply illusion.

◆ ◆ ◆

The place of unknowing is one of the most powerful destinations in the universe.

♦ ♦ ♦

Don't just light your own fire.

Be the spark that sets the world ablaze, one that reaches into the depths of humanity to go where no soul has ventured before.

Be the spark that encourages evolution over dissolution, love over hate, equality over separation, forgiveness over resentment. Be the spark that reaches into the heavens so that the gods take notice.

And once they do, you won't need to light your own fire. The privileges bestowed upon you for your selflessness will have you burning so brightly that you yourself will have evolved into a blessing on earth.

♦ ♦ ♦

She wiped her tears only to realize they weren't rolling down her cheeks but from her ancestor standing beside her.

She turned around and bowed her head to honor the long-held grief in her lineage, now recognizing it as a strength instead of a weakness. Each thread you carry has lived a life before you. Carry it sacredly, for it will teach you about your journey.

♦ ♦ ♦

The elder looked at the child and desired to remember his own innocence. The child gazed at the elder and hoped for his wisdom. The gods laughed in amusement. Those who are truly wise never lose their innocence. And for those who remain innocent, wisdom finds them without ever having to search for it.

♦ ♦ ♦

Yesterday I needed to get out for some supplies and much needed fresh air. It was raining off and on here in New York, a much-needed respite given from nature's tears to both replenish and cleanse impurities amidst us. I took a detour to one of my favorite places in Westchester: a few towns along the Hudson River culminating in one of the most powerful portals I have ever embraced here on the East Coast. Many times, another sensitive friend and I have driven there to simply bask in its energies of healing and grace. As we were driving through one of the towns, we passed a burial ground, and I could not believe my eyes. Spirits were dancing amidst the ground in large numbers, rejoicing as though they had just been freed. I opened my window, as I could see them as plainly as I could see myself, and kept waving. I know it sounds funny, but I had never witnessed such a mass exodus of souls from one plane/dimension to another in such a way. I have seen smaller shifts in the spirit world like this before, but something was different; something was very palpably different. They were free from their present state of manifestation and heading toward the next level of their spiritual destiny; the leniency granted was so profound I just kept reminding myself of the prayers of mercy I used to pray for those departed who were stuck or simply waiting for familial miasms to heal so that they might move on. Many traditions pray and hold ceremony for the departed to ask for graces and prayers from the unseen. If ever you needed a time to both ask for help and show gratitude toward your loved ones who are beyond the veil, now would be it. I promise you, their prayers have just become all the more powerful. Amen.

◆ ◆ ◆

And come twilight, the heavens will descend on us with such a roar that all of Creation will understand the miracles that have awakened us.

◆ ◆ ◆

In this time of physical, emotional, and spiritual inconvenience, God is creating a new language for humanity, one in which we have the slightest awareness of the mercy that awaits us.

◆ ◆ ◆

What an extraordinarily powerful wind last night here in New York City. I went out to bear witness to the magnificence of its purpose. A wind like that is deserving of such reverence and humility, as it carries souls from this world to the next. Such rawness with which it carries emotions of those who have perished in this pandemic and those who are crying for their lost loved ones. Every tear is held in its powerful grace. Every anger soothed; every fear comforted.

The wind is still strong this morning, flitting from this world to the next with such swiftness, as called to by the gods of Creation. I keep hearing the words, "Forgive us our trespasses." The heavens have given us such an opportunity during this time to explore our relationship to forgiveness. Forgiving ourselves and those who have hurt us, and forgiving the unknown, the unseen, and a voice that has no name in our minds but is understood by all of Creation. Thank you, wind, for carrying many of your children home. Amen.

◆ ◆ ◆

Bless those whose enormous courage rivals that of any angel in heaven.

They are the chosen ones, those who have sacrificed their earthly experience during this time of crisis to enter into the world beyond the veil for the sake of humanity.

Their purpose is not lost, for it has finally been found,

Their pasts forgotten to innocence and humility as God

awaits them at those heavenly doors, forgiving all misgivings upon their earthly embodiment.

They are the awakened ones, the ones whose prayers of hope and mercy will humble this pandemic until it settles into grace.

They are the awakened ones, the ones who will hold our hands in times of great fear and doubt, in times of despair and isolation.

They are the awakened ones, the ones who will unite us in a way humanity has never known before.

There is a purpose to their sacrifice, to their suffering, to our loss.

A purpose that we cannot explain or comprehend in our hearts at this moment in time,

But one we will come to understand as time passes.

Bless those whose enormous courage rivals that of any angel in heaven.

Humanity will forever be indebted by their passage of grace.

We are no longer standing at the threshold. We have become the threshold. Allow evolution to pass through you as gently as you can, carrying yourself amidst the anguish of humanity, only to see yourself eventually rise along with it. And yes, you will rise. We all will.

◆ ◆ ◆

Bless you, wind outside my window. I went out for a moment to feel your immense courage and strength, acting as a psychopomp, crossing souls from one world to the next. There are many souls in your bosom today, dear wind, so much so that when I stood still outside I tingled as they passed through me, illuminating my own etheric body. What do you have to teach me today, wind? Your might is fierce, perhaps even leaving behind some destruction in the wake of your path. But I do not fear you, as your purpose is great—to raise these souls from suffering and bring them to the holy land of peace eternal. I do hear the confusion of those souls as they are crossing. I have been hearing it through my prayers this morning with clients. May their confusion and ours be comforted by faith and by a warmth that only the Divine can ignite. When you hear the wind today, please say a prayer for those crossing. Your own heaviness will begin to lift. Amen.

◆ ◆ ◆

It is during this time that our innate sacred power will be revealed to us. A power that will exemplify a justice to be bestowed by the gods of heaven, one that will ignite humanity to cultivate a greater sense of compassion and humility more than ever before. This power will carry equal merit among every human being, leaving no one without dignity or grace—no one. We have been asked to carry this torch since time birthed itself into Creation, but our own unworthiness instilled fear into our hearts and minds. This torch, this light for humanity, is indeed ready to be lit in ways unimaginable. Gather yourselves, gather your children, gather your friends and neighbors. The gods await our resurrection and the evolution toward a kinder, gentler, and more forgiving human experience.

◆ ◆ ◆

My Prayer for the Anniversary of September 11

I remember the souls passing through my walls for weeks before. I remember the voices, the screams, the fire. I remember not understanding what I was seeing. The human carnage appearing rampant between the worlds. I also remember my rosary, my holy books, my prayers in any tradition I knew. I remember as many angels as there were spirits, who were stunned at what just happened to them. I remember as many guardians and elementals in various dimensions coming together to help the wounded, more than I will probably ever see again in one lifetime. I remember seeing the ineffable light, more brilliant than any darkness that appeared. For anyone who doubts what I am about to share, please consider my words. Since I was young and had these abilities, one of the greatest graces I have been afforded was the privilege to see and know that souls are taken out of their bodies before a trauma of any magnitude occurs. I was praying for many weeks and working with the souls of September 11 before it happened. I know there were many others with the same experience.

There is a merciful Creator who carries us within the womb of Divine Providence, where we are sheltered against the storms of tragedy. For those who continue to hold on to the traumatic pattern of the suffering surrounding the events of September 11, the greatest gift you can offer those beyond the veil is the gift of letting go. Collectively, if we can see the light as I know many of them have, we can raise the vibration of the collective trauma to something we can all come to peace with in time. Our understanding and internal dialogue surrounding the tragic experience still needs much healing. Every anniversary, I sit back and remember those souls and the fear I felt at not knowing what was about to happen. I pause. And then I remember those angels, those helping spirits, those who came to comfort the lost weeks before the event actually took place. I remember when the healing began, the love and presence of the Creator I felt to help guide the way of all those who were in darkness. If I continue to look at the events in darkness, I don't think it will serve those continuing to heal in both worlds. I want to remember the light amidst the darkness, the grace amidst the tragedy.

◆ ◆ ◆

Beyond all comprehension you will find the answers you seek. Not in words that fulfill false expectations, but in moments of Presence when you stand at the threshold of who you are in this very moment in time. Nothing can take that away from you, for that moment is divinely bestowed. As mighty as the archangels of heaven, that Presence will keep you safe, more so than you could ever know.

◆ ◆ ◆

In remembrance of the oppressed of every nation whose footprints walked this gentle earth, help us to honor, oh ancestors, each suffering, each grave that carries the tears of those tormented by human iniquities. May their perseverance and might pave the way for humility amidst the human condition. May we be unburdened of false truths so that we stand together in compassionate unity. Those beyond the veil, forgive us for not understanding that your suffering is our suffering, that your oppression has become our oppression, that trauma repeats itself until we cultivate a mercy toward humanity that we have never known. Only then will we be free. Amen.

◆ ◆ ◆

The echo of loneliness is such an intimate experience for each of us struggling through this time.

No words or deeds can carry us from this darkness into the light. Only Divine Presence can shelter us from ourselves, from the inner storm that transcends loneliness into a darkness most of us are overwhelmed by. It is a path we must walk graciously and forgivingly within ourselves. Our loneliness needs our forgiveness. It needs our understanding, and it needs our patience. It needs nourishment to awaken to a reality beyond human comprehension, beyond an identity that furthers the illusion that we are all separate. I am asking you to forgive the illusion, so that the inherent light that loneliness carries will shower you with grace.

♦ ♦ ♦

As we shine a light in the darkness during this time, we have to own that we are a part of the darkness, at times desire it, use it for our own advantage, and manipulate it to hurt others. All of us, individually and collectively. From the graves of our ancestors to the wounding of humanity, may this crisis allow us to see the depths of who we really are and what we need to do to foster forgiveness and truth amidst change.

♦ ♦ ♦

When this is over, you are not returning to the world. You are returning to yourself, in ways you could never imagine.

♦ ♦ ♦

Our collective moral compass will be elevated not by any political strategy to alleviate the human condition at this time in history, but by any act of compassionate human decency we can offer one another. Mercy is more triumphant in times of suffering when actions do not yield an outcome we hope to achieve.

♦ ♦ ♦

Oh, great rain, your brilliant sojourn in this realm today left me speechless.

Dancing upon the earth while whispering between the shadows of the ethers, you illuminated my senses with such purification that I can't help but contain myself. I wanted to dance naked while each raindrop pressed against my flesh in sacred harmony against a windswept backdrop of merciful revelations only the quietest of souls could hear. I pray you let me dance with you the next time you visit, for you cleanse me of iniquities I no longer need to carry on this earth. May your holiness become my holiness, oh blessed waters from the sky above.

◆ ◆ ◆

And as you surrender, the land beneath your feet will become holy ground, not as you have known it in the past but as you envision it for your future and for those souls waiting to be born.

◆ ◆ ◆

And the tree whispered in my ear,

"Thank you for remembering the sacred silence, this time of respite toward the earth, with humanity standing still as we grieve together the pain of our world. We need this time to rest gently and to become acquainted with one another again as equals under the sun."

◆ ◆ ◆

The ancestral keepers of the earth are awakening in multitudes as humanity is stilled for a while. May their perseverance in mending the wounds of our home be given the time and respect it deserves.

◆ ◆ ◆

You fly not because you have wings but because you believe you can.

◆ ◆ ◆

Settling into grace, I become myself.

◆ ◆ ◆

True enlightenment doesn't seek wisdom. It seeks a stillness beyond any comprehension wisdom could hope to attain.

◆ ◆ ◆

"I don't know."

One of the most powerful statements in the universe.

It can bring human beings to their knees in desperation or raise them to the heights of the gods. In my work for almost twenty-four years now, I have been privileged and humbled to be able to afford answers to life's challenges, whether they be physical , spiritual, emotional, or ancestral in nature. One of the greatest gifts I have been given and am able to pass on to others is when I answer a client's question with "I don't know."

I have learned to breathe so much easier when that response comes across my lips. It takes a few moments, after utilizing every source within me to assist someone. And then it happens. Miraculously. A grace descends on me, the gods bring me to my own silence, and there is no answer. I breathe deeply. I used to search for words of comfort before responding with this statement, but I have learned to become very okay with "I don't know" over these years. The response from most people is the same at first. The chest tightens, the breathing slows down, the perplexed facial expression—even when I work via phone I can sense the same reaction. It is usually met with another question in return. How could I not know? So I sit with them in the unknown. Yes, at times I still offer comfort, but at other times I reiterate, "I just don't know." I verbalize it with a firm gentleness and pay close attention to their breathing, their cellular responses, their energy fields. I wait with them. We wait in the silence together for that same grace to descend on us as a whole, so that in the unknown they can feel the grace of God surrounding them. What was once a response born out of desperation to my statement becomes something much more powerful for the other person. Something empowering. Something strengthening. Something humbling.

So I will leave you all with a few words.

I just don't know.

◆ ◆ ◆

The rain is coming down hard tonight here in New York. There is no softness in its temperament. Its voice is so loud the echoes of what used to be are taking on physical form, compelling me to seek refuge and gentleness amidst the unknown. There is a weariness to its voice. And as I write this, spirits are walking behind me through the portals that have been opening and are available to all of us during this time. I don't know how many of you have carried a heavy heart this week, but some of those souls near to me are whispering words of regret, time lost—similar energies to the pounding rain right outside my door right now. There is one specific male soul around me from long ago, connected to those crossing over during this pandemic. The others continue to "walk" by me. His regrets have become his identity beyond the veil, stuck in between realms, hardened by his earthly experience while here. I am telling him to cross with the others, to allow the rain to lift his bitterness so that his regrets soften and perhaps take refuge in a new realm of possibility. Refuge. Love that word. Whether it is refuge amidst the unknown or refuge in the pounding rain, may it soften us and all those regrets we carry until we meet that sacred refuge that lives within each and every one of us.

◆ ◆ ◆

There are days I long to be a wildflower, with beams of radiant sunlight on my face, rooted in the earth ever so gently, comforted by my wildflower companions.

Basking in the glow of nature surrounding me, only to hear myself whisper to God, "Thank you."

◆ ◆ ◆

We are not reentering our world; we are reentering ourselves.

◆ ◆ ◆

When enlightened ones look to find your darkness, they know not to go further than to look amidst your light. One cannot survive without the other until stillness reigns truth within the haven of your soul.

◆ ◆ ◆

In times of individual and collective trauma, it is as normal to question our courage as it is to question our fear. We cannot define our relationship to courage according to another's experiences or expectations. Nor is it appropriate to judge how others respond to trauma, as it is inherently a solo journey.

◆ ◆ ◆

Being motivated by truth can be challenging when we all see through our own lens of life experiences. Sometimes we have to take a step back and allow for other truths to be ignited that have never even crossed our paths, so that a collective truth, one that serves a purpose even greater than the one we originally held, may avail itself.

◆ ◆ ◆

Sometimes humanity needs a little chaos so it can truly appreciate the privilege of what life has to offer.

◆ ◆ ◆

You beautiful, wounded soul.

Soon you will be marching to the beat of your own drum, as driven by the symphony of the gods whispering into your ear over and over again,

"There will never be a time when you and I are parted. Your soul is my soul, and my soul abounds in all realms of that which is seen and unseen. The music you hear will be like none other in the universe. The beat of your drum will echo the beat of your replenished heart, a heart among many, touched by a vast universe that only knows love."

◆ ◆ ◆

The reintegration of a unified collective is happening now in the spirit world.

Beyond the veil, miasms are being either strengthened or broken.

In other dimensions, this is not about the political climate but about darkness and light in its purest form.

What we do with the information that comes our way as a result of the political climate will alter our genetic history both past and present.

In this world, for many right now, their identities are aligned with who win elections.

Beyond the veil, it is about making amends for past grievances, releasing old trauma, forgiveness.

Great acts of forgiveness can change any world.

No matter the outcome, a deeper inner work has begun.

◆ ◆ ◆

Your last dance belongs to the gods, so make the song of your life an extraordinary one.

◆ ◆ ◆

Your story is not ending during this crisis. It is being rewritten. Your grief, your worry, your fears can all be transcribed into glorious poetry, unfolding with each moment as Divine Intervention takes hold of your words and carries them further into relationship with yourself than you ever thought possible. Your story will be miraculous. Tend to it with reverence.

◆ ◆ ◆

So many people question what exists for them beyond the veil when they cross. Yet when they finally reach that threshold, they look back and question what existed for them while they were here.

Make every embodied moment matter so that when you live among the clouds, you will remember your human experience with such reverence.

8

HEALING VOICES
FROM THE PANDEMIC

Twenty twenty was the year that changed our hearts and our lives forever. The Coronavirus pandemic represented a current in our psychic and physical spheres of reality that challenged our internal definitions of both the light and the darkness. It compelled us into stillness as much as it compelled us into chaos. The boundaries we identified our existences with no longer wove a humanity that was recognizable. The pandemic needed a voice. Humanity needed a voice. Our suffering needed a voice. And in those voices, the words that follow in this chapter flowed through my hands in an effort to be a bridge for healing.

Dear Corona,

It's been a while since I've written a letter and felt compelled to reach out.

I don't know you personally, but rest assured my ancestors knew your ancestors both in times of great strength and in great weakness.

You have given me ample opportunity to pause and reflect. And for this, I am grateful.

My reflections have become so sacred and filled with gratitude for all that you are teaching me—all that you are teaching us.

I know you are in a time of exploring your own inner darkness as well as your light, and you have given humanity the distinct opportunity to do the same.

If your intention was to alienate and isolate human beings into a confounded state of oblivion, you have done the opposite, dear friend.

I have seen more stars at night yearning to come out in the day to guide us in our times of fear. I have witnessed more rainbows amidst the natural world, as the earth's manifestations take respite under God's care from man's recklessness. I watch as the sky settles into grace, as the soil once again nourishes plant life in a way that it has not done before. This rest you are providing us is regenerating the earth and its inhabitants. Squirrels are dancing once again; trees are praying in unison. Oh, how I marvel at the miracles you have created.

You do not discriminate via race, religion, social status; my list could go on. How wise of you to share with us that grief, fear, and anger, and every emotion under the rainbow embraces each of us equally. That suffering is inclusive, and not exclusive of identity or purpose. In fact, you have ignited an even greater purpose in our minds and hearts and within the collective of the human construct. We as a world identity created such boundaries to keep us separate from one another, competing for self-worth and power, forgetting humility and honor many times. That is all changing now. We are beginning to see how those boundaries are self-limiting, self-destructive, and within ourselves foster an even greater sense of separation.

Even those who are beyond the veil are gathering

in prayer and celebration during this time of evolution.

Tears flow down my cheeks as families spend more time with each other, relearning the art of communication and intimacy. Emotions once internalized have a safe outlet to be shared. Entitlement is being humbled in dramatic ways. Love is being explored to such depths that we will come out as better human beings than we were before. Rest is being taken that never sees the light of day. You are showing us it is not us versus them anymore, but us, just us. Finally. Tears again.

For those whose lives you are taking, they are so not alone as they transition. Our prayers have raised them to such heights that angels await their last breath to carry them home upon their wings. You have brought us many gifts, Corona, coming into our homes uninvited, or were you uninvited? Sometimes I wonder.

I wish you well on your journey to find the light.

And one day, perhaps we will meet as different souls on the journey.

Until you find stillness,
Laura

◆ ◆ ◆

The year ahead is the year of reckoning. Not one of punishment, but of realignment to a reality where the collective has the opportunity to embrace forgiveness to such a degree that we will know loss in ways unknown to us before. Loss of self and our perceptions of who we think we are within the emptiness, the pain, the unknown, and in our quest for enlightenment.

The Divine will command an intensity of stillness that will envelop us in rapture more than any other time in history. The thread of humanity will no longer carry individual needs to the heavens as we understand them, but collective wounds embracing all living things will create the new alignment. For some of us, it will feel like such a power struggle, exhausting every bone in our bodies as we expend mental energy in wanting to understand the Divine's every move.

The Year of Reckoning will compel us to come together because of the loss we will experience on both personal and collective levels. There is beauty in this loss, a holiness that we have never experienced before and can only do so once we surrender. We will expand into forgiveness with more ease and a grace that will give humanity the opportunity to love to a greater capacity than we thought we were ever capable of.

◆ ◆ ◆

All viruses have an innate intelligence.

They are as old as time itself and are a part of an ever-changing ecosystem that enters a host and attaches itself in various ways to cellular membrane as its genetic imprint forms a relationship. The way it will influence its host depends on many factors from emotional and environmental to spiritual and other epigenetic influences.

Viruses contain DNA and RNA, just as we do. Its intelligence is far reaching. It knows how to survive better than most humans do. It knows how to replicate, transmit, and cross system boundaries on many levels. From my perspective, its skill set is pretty impressive, and we could learn a lot from this living intelligence.

Throughout history we have created personal and interdependent relationships with viruses, and in my work for over twenty-four years, I have seen viral threads in people's epigenetic fields from their ancestry still influencing current-day illnesses. I've also seen viruses react to certain frequencies. As times change, viruses and our relationship to them within our bodies change.

From a psychological and spiritual perspective, fear is a valid response but one on which a virus can also replicate itself energetically. I am watching how, both personally and collectively, we as a society are dramatizing the pandemic. Don't get me wrong, precautions are warranted; but the truth of the matter is viruses will exist until the end of time. Most of us carry viral threads and don't even know we have them. Many of us have been exposed to viruses from our ancestors, and those viruses live in our bodies. My own great-grandmother died in the epidemic of the Spanish flu.

The dramatization of any crisis comes in part out of fear of the unknown, our relationship to both power and powerlessness, and within our ability to have a relationship with illness itself. Civilizations have faced pandemics and the loss of life since we evolved into being. There is a necessary life cycle for viruses and their counterparts just as there is for humanity. Hard to accept but all of Creation breeds intelligent life-forms that might threaten our very existence. My own approach has been to have a conversation with the virus, as I do whenever I fall ill to a viral syndrome, and find out what it needs from me and, possibly, what I might learn from it. A virus is not something, in my belief, that we can truly eradicate as a whole. It can be contained. There is a difference.

The environment we live in also plays a role in helping viruses to spread. When I used to do hands-on work eons ago, I would watch viruses in my clients run away from my hands.

Research done on viruses suggests they are contained by higher frequencies of light. When Rife machines were popular, people believed in the efficacy of their frequencies to match those of many pathogens. Many living things in nature have high frequencies. Prayer has a high frequency.

While the media is speaking of prevention, I am not hearing anything about how 5G, increased use of pesticides, spreading GMOs, and so on are contributing to weakened bio-immunity and the altering of DNA.

Much of humanity enjoys an easier life, unfortunately without consideration that our food supply, the air we breathe, technology, all impact our DNA at a cellular level. Thus, new viruses will be born and old ones will be resurrected. This is and will be the nature of things.

I'm sitting back and taking some precautions, but also opening up dialogue with Coronavirus to see what it has to teach humanity at this point in time. I send my love and respect toward nature, for our not understanding or respecting the many forms of intelligence it breeds and wanting to eradicate anything that poses a threat, which in the long run might serve us in ways we have yet to see. We cannot control the circle of life, folks. We can learn to be in relationship with it as best we can.

◆ ◆ ◆

The lower levels of the spirit world are mirroring what is happening within the human collective right now.

The terror has become greater than the pandemic itself.

I feel I need to say that again to offer the miasm some space:

The terror has become greater than the pandemic itself.

Please don't get me wrong. Fear is an appropriate psychological and emotional response to any threat or crisis. I am not going to ask you to replace fear with love. I just won't do that. I am going to ask you to hold space for both, to allow both possibilities to exist as you compartmentalize and internalize your reactions and responses to what is happening out there.

The fear has now taken on form, an energy form that is just as intrusive on our boundary systems as is the Coronavirus. Even with social distancing, there are enough people in the world that no one has to struggle alone with this—no one. One can even help others through prayer.

We are all working diligently to respect social distancing. So what about enacting psychological, spiritual, and emotional distancing from those thoughts and reactions that are furthering you into the abyss?

There are things each of us can do to help ourselves and each other. The act of creation is our birthright.

The act and art of acceptance is also our birthright.

I see the light at the end of the tunnel.

I see the darkness even before we got to this place.

If we can create healthier relationships to our desperation, our powerlessness, our terror, we can shift some things here for everyone.

As human beings, we do not like to feel powerless. We have a hard time embracing suffering. We want to be in control of everything.

The us versus them paradigm can no longer survive in this new world being created, but we won't learn that lesson until we each explore our own relationships with power and powerlessness. Loss happens. It is happening. It will happen. We are each being faced with the loss of our personal identities, our roles in society, and how we see others. What is on the other side of that has the opportunity of being miraculous, but that will not change the fact that much loss will occur. And with that comes an intensity of grief and emptiness we have never allowed ourselves to experience before.

I am with you.

We are all with you.

May we cherish the opportunity to pray collectively for each other through these times.

Amen.

◆ ◆ ◆

Every last bit of healing medicine surrounding this pandemic will be passed down to future generations. Your children's children will remember how you responded to this time—physically, emotionally, and spiritually. It will influence how they respond in the face of crisis, and that in turn will influence their children. It's called epigenetics.

Let's show them what we're made of.

◆ ◆ ◆

I view Coronavirus as one of the greatest portals toward evolution of this century. Yes, many lives are being taken. But in truth, most of us are being given life. A life that we never knew existed before. An opportunity to love like no other and to care for humanity and the earth in unprecedented ways. Embrace its teachings.

◆ ◆ ◆

My Last Breath

I need for you to know I was not alone.

I could barely catch my breath. With every inhalation, memories of you would flood my mind—your smile, your warmth, our lives together. It made me pause and stripped away any fear I had about being isolated, waiting for that breath to fill me until I exhaled with relief. I knew my time was coming. You may not have been there, but everyone we know who had already made their way across worlds was by my side. I laughed as I watched souls reach for my hand to comfort me, some I had actually never even met. I knew they had succumbed to the same dire consequences as I did. I was part of this collective crossing of souls to such a degree that I was beginning to understand its purpose. Family members, friends, strangers—all in spirit form—gathered as I struggled for air and realized there was no way that any of us would ever be left to cross alone. The laughter emanating from these souls made me forget the loud noises surrounding me from my hospital room, the machines I am hooked up to, the heavy energy and stench of fear that I felt when I was first brought here.

I'm taking my last breath now. I can see the angels parting those around me to reassure me of my ascent.

Oh, how blessed I am to be part of this calling, this mass evolution that will help heal humanity in ways I don't even understand quite yet. Their wings are so effervescent I can hardly contain myself. I'm lifting, I'm lifting. Boy, I wish you could see me fly. I wish you could feel how so untethered I am from everything that weighed me down. I wish you could know how many of us beyond the veil are praying for you all. What's happening to humanity is not what you think. I wish the angels would explain it to me so you would all suffer less until this has passed. But they won't. So I can't.

I'm sorry I left you too soon, but if you could only see this other world you would understand why. I am but a whisper away, helping you work through your fear of the unknown and the plethora of emotions you are still feeling along with everyone else trying to make sense of the world right now. Humanity will be so different. The angels are jumping for joy at what will come. But I do know that a number of us had to cross worlds to prepare the way for you, and I was chosen as one of them. And just so you know, I would do it all over again because that is how much I love you.